SIDE *by* SIDES

PRESTWICK HOUSE, INC.

TWELFTH NIGHT;

OR, WHAT YOU WILL

WILLIAM SHAKESPEARE

Shakespeare's text

on the left;

a modern rendering

on the right.

Prestwick House

P.O. Box 658 • Clayton, DE 19938
Tel: 1.800.932.4593
Web site: www.prestwickhouse.com

ISBN 978 1-58049-511-0

Table of Contents

DRAMATIS PERSONAE

ORSINO, Duke of Illyria.

SEBASTIAN, brother to Viola.

ANTONIO, a sea captain, friend to Sebastian.

A Sea Captain, friend to Viola.

VALENTINE, gentleman attending on the Duke.

CURIO, gentleman attending on the Duke.

SIR TOBY BELCH, uncle to Olivia.

SIR ANDREW AGUECHEEK, Sir Toby's friend.

MALVOLIO, steward to Olivia.

FABIAN, servant to Olivia.

FESTE, a Clown, servant to Olivia.

OLIVIA.

VIOLA.

MARIA, Olivia's maid.

Lords, Priests, Sailors, Officers, Musicians, and other Attendants.

SCENE: A city in Illyria, and the seacoast near it.

ACT I

SCENE 1
Duke Orsino's palace.

[Enter Duke Orsino, Curio, and other Lords; Musicians attending]

DUKE ORSINO: If music be the food of love, play on;
    Give me excess of it, that, surfeiting,
    The appetite may sicken, and so die.
    That strain again! it had a dying fall:
5   O, it came o'er my ear like the sweet sound,
    That breathes upon a bank of violets,
    Stealing and giving odour! Enough; no more:
    'Tis not so sweet now as it was before.
    O spirit of love! how quick and fresh art thou,
10   That, notwithstanding thy capacity
    Receiveth as the sea, nought enters there,
    Of what validity and pitch soe'er,
    But falls into abatement and low price,
    Even in a minute: so full of shapes is fancy
15   That it alone is high fantastical.

CURIO: Will you go hunt, my lord?

DUKE ORSINO: What, CURIO?

CURIO: The hart.

ACT I

SCENE 1
An apartment in the Duke's palace.

[Enter Duke, Curio, and other Lords; Musicians following and performing.]

DUKE: *If music feeds love, keep playing. Give me too much of it, so that, by overindulging in it, my desire for it will lessen and end. Play that chord again! It had a mournful tone. Oh, I heard it like the sweet sound that lingers about a bank of violets, while the flowers absorb the surrounding odors and give off their own. Stop playing it now. It is not as sweet as it was before. Oh, spirit of love, you are so full of life and hungry! Although you can hold as much as the sea, nothing comes to you, no matter what its value, without immediately becoming diminished and worthless. Love is so full of assortments that it is completely an illusion.*

CURIO: *Would you like to go hunting, my lord?*

DUKE: *Hunting for what, Curio?*

CURIO: *The hart.*

DUKE ORSINO: Why, so I do, the noblest that I have:
20 O, when mine eyes did see Olivia first,
 Methought she purged the air of pestilence!
 That instant was I turn'd into a hart;
 And my desires, like fell and cruel hounds,
 E'er since pursue me.

[Enter Valentine]
25 How now! what news from her?

VALENTINE: So please my lord, I might not be admitted;
 But from her handmaid do return this answer:
 The element itself, till seven years' heat,
 Shall not behold her face at ample view;
30 But, like a cloistress, she will veiled walk
 And water once a day her chamber round
 With eye-offending brine: all this to season
 A brother's dead love, which she would keep fresh
 And lasting in her sad remembrance.

35 **DUKE ORSINO:** O, she that hath a heart of that fine frame
 To pay this debt of love but to a brother,
 How will she love, when the rich golden shaft
 Hath kill'd the flock of all affections else
 That live in her; when liver, brain and heart,
40 These sovereign thrones, are all supplied, and fill'd
 Her sweet perfections with one self king!
 Away before me to sweet beds of flowers:
 Love-thoughts lie rich when canopied with bowers.

[Exeunt]

DUKE: *That is what I am doing; it is the most valuable that I have. Oh, when I first saw Olivia, I thought she made the air pure. That moment I became a hart, and my desires, like fierce and cruel hounds, have chased me ever since.*

[Enter Valentine.]
    How are you? What news do you have from her?

VALENTINE: *My Lord, I was not asked in, but her servant gave me this answer. For the next seven years, the sky itself will not fully see her face. She will walk veiled like a nun and cry once a day in her room. She is doing all this to honor the love of her dead brother, which she wants to keep clear and lasting in her sad remembering.*

DUKE: *Oh, the woman who has such a good heart that she shows this much love for just a brother, imagine how she will love when Cupid's arrow has struck and killed all the affections she feels for others. Imagine how she will love when her usually separate feelings, her passions, thoughts, and love, are united and ruled by one desire that satisfies her needs and completes her sweet perfection. Take me to the flower garden. Thoughts of love are nurtured by the outdoors.*

[They exit.]

SCENE 2
The sea-coast.

[Enter Viola:, a Captain, and Sailors]

VIOLA: What country, friends, is this?

CAPTAIN: This is Illyria, lady.

VIOLA: And what should I do in Illyria?
My brother he is in Elysium.
5   Perchance he is not drown'd: what think you, sailors?

CAPTAIN: It is perchance that you yourself were saved.

VIOLA: O my poor brother! and so perchance may he be.

CAPTAIN: True, madam: and, to comfort you with chance,
Assure yourself, after our ship did split,
10   When you and those poor number saved with you
Hung on our driving boat, I saw your brother,
Most provident in peril, bind himself,
Courage and hope both teaching him the practise,
To a strong mast that lived upon the sea;
15   Where, like Arion on the dolphin's back,
I saw him hold acquaintance with the waves
So long as I could see.

VIOLA: For saying so, there's gold:
Mine own escape unfoldeth to my hope,
20   Whereto thy speech serves for authority,
The like of him. Know'st thou this country?

CAPTAIN: Ay, madam, well; for I was bred and born
Not three hours' travel from this very place.

VIOLA: Who governs here?

SCENE 2
The sea coast.

[Enter Viola, a Captain, and Sailors.]

VIOLA: *What country is this, my friends?*

CAPTAIN: *This is Illyria, lady.*

VIOLA: *What am I doing in Illyria? My brother is in heaven. Maybe, by chance, he did not drown. What do you think, sailors?*

CAPTAIN: *It is only by chance that you were saved.*

VIOLA: *Oh, my poor brother! Perhaps he was saved, too.*

CAPTAIN: *True, madam. To comfort you with chance, I will assure you. After our ship split, when you, and those poor people saved with you, held onto our drifting boat, I saw your brother acting wisely in the face of danger. He bound himself with courage and hope to a floating piece of the wreckage. He held on in the waves, like Arion on the dolphin's back, for as long as I could see him.*

VIOLA: *For telling me that, I will pay you. My own escape gives me hope that he survived, and your story strengthens this hope. Do you know this country?*

CAPTAIN: *I know it well, madam, because I was born and raised about 3 hours from here.*

VIOLA: *Who rules this land?*

25   CAPTAIN: A noble duke, in nature as in name.

VIOLA: What is the name?

CAPTAIN: Orsino.

VIOLA: Orsino! I have heard my father name him:
He was a bachelor then.

30   CAPTAIN: And so is now, or was so very late;
For but a month ago I went from hence,
And then 'twas fresh in murmur,—as, you know,
What great ones do the less will prattle of,—
That he did seek the love of fair Olivia.

35   VIOLA: What's she?

CAPTAIN: A virtuous maid, the daughter of a count
That died some twelvemonth since, then leaving her
In the protection of his son, her brother,
Who shortly also died: for whose dear love,
40   They say, she hath abjured the company
And sight of men.

VIOLA: O that I served that lady
And might not be delivered to the world,
Till I had made mine own occasion mellow,
45   What my estate is!

CAPTAIN: That were hard to compass;
Because she will admit no kind of suit,
No, not the duke's.

VIOLA: There is a fair behavior in thee, captain;
50   And though that nature with a beauteous wall
Doth oft close in pollution, yet of thee
I will believe thou hast a mind that suits
With this thy fair and outward character.

CAPTAIN: *A duke, who is noble by both nature and birth.*

VIOLA: *What is his name?*

CAPTAIN: *Orsino.*

VIOLA: *Orsino! I have heard my father talk about him. He was a bachelor back then.*

CAPTAIN: *He still is, or still was not long ago. About a month ago, I left here, and there was gossip, (because, as you know, what the nobility does the commoners will talk about), that he was seeking the love of the beautiful Olivia.*

VIOLA: *Who is she?*

CAPTAIN: *She is a respectable woman and the daughter of a count, who died a year ago. He left her in the protection of his son, her brother, who died shortly after. They say she has sworn off the company and sight of men in honor of her brother's dear love.*

VIOLA: *I wish I could serve this lady in order to keep my name and rank a secret, until I choose to make it known.*

CAPTAIN: *That would be hard to accomplish, because she will not speak with anyone, not even the Duke.*

VIOLA: *You seem to be a good man, Captain. Although nature sometimes conceals pollution with a beautiful outward appearance, I believe you have a mind that matches your noble façade. I ask you, and I will pay you greatly, conceal what I am, and help me take on the disguise that best serves my purpose. I will serve this duke. You will present me to him as*

55

I prithee, and I'll pay thee bounteously,
Conceal me what I am, and be my aid
For such disguise as haply shall become
The form of my intent. I'll serve this duke:
Thou shall present me as an eunuch to him:
It may be worth thy pains; for I can sing

60

And speak to him in many sorts of music
That will allow me very worth his service.
What else may hap to time I will commit;
Only shape thou thy silence to my wit.

CAPTAIN: Be you his eunuch, and your mute I'll be:

65

When my tongue blabs, then let mine eyes not see.

VIOLA: I thank thee: lead me on.   *[Exeunt]*

SCENE 3
Olivia's house.

[Enter Sir Toby Belch and Maris]

SIR TOBY: What a plague means my niece, to take the death of
her brother thus? I am sure care's an enemy to life.

MARIA: By my troth, Sir Toby, you must come in earlier o' nights:
your cousin, my lady, takes great exceptions to your ill hours.

5

SIR TOBY: Why, let her except, before excepted.

MARIA: Ay, but you must confine yourself within the modest
limits of order.

SIR TOBY: Confine! I'll confine myself no finer than I am: these
clothes are good enough to drink in; and so be these boots

10

too: an they be not, let them hang themselves in their own
straps.

16

a eunuch. It will be worth your efforts, because I can sing and speak to him in many sorts of music that will make me a worthy servant. We will have to wait and see what else happens, but keep quiet until I say so.

CAPTAIN: *You will be his eunuch, and I will be your mute. If I give away your secrets, let me go blind.*

VIOLA: *Thank you. Lead me on.*   [They exit.]

SCENE 3
Olivia's house.

[Enter Sir Toby Belch and Maris]

SIR TOBY: *Why is my niece taking her brother's death so hard? I am sure worry is bad for one's health.*

MARIA: *By heaven, Sir Toby, you must come home earlier at night. Your niece, the woman I serve, takes great exception to your late hours.*

SIR TOBY: *Well let her except, as long as I am one of her exceptions.*

MARIA: *Yes, but you must confine yourself to decent and acceptable behavior.*

SIR TOBY: *Confine! I will confine myself to no finer finery than I am wearing. These clothes are good enough to drink in and so are these boots. If they are not, let them hang themselves by their own shoelaces.*

MARIA: That quaffing and drinking will undo you: I heard my lady talk of it yesterday; and of a foolish knight that you brought in one night here to be her wooer.

15 SIR TOBY: Who, Sir Andrew Aguecheek?

MARIA: Ay, he.

SIR TOBY: He's as tall a man as any's in Illyria.

MARIA: What's that to the purpose?

SIR TOBY: Why, he has three thousand ducats a year.

20 MARIA: Ay, but he'll have but a year in all these ducats: he's a very fool and a prodigal.

SIR TOBY: Fie, that you'll say so! he plays o' the viol-de-gamboys, and speaks three or four languages word for word without book, and hath all the good gifts of nature.

25 MARIA: He hath indeed, almost natural: for besides that he's a fool, he's a great quarreller: and but that he hath the gift of a coward to allay the gust he hath in quarrelling, 'tis thought among the prudent he would quickly have the gift of a grave.

SIR TOBY: By this hand, they are scoundrels and subtractors that
30 say so of him. Who are they?

MARIA: They that add, moreover, he's drunk nightly in your company.

SIR TOBY: With drinking healths to my niece: I'll drink to her as long as there is a passage in my throat and drink in Illyria:
35 he's a coward and a coystrill that will not drink to my niece till his brains turn o' the toe like a parish-top. What, wench! Castiliano vulgo! for here comes Sir Andrew Agueface.

MARIA: *That drinking will ruin your life. I heard Olivia talking about it yesterday and about a foolish knight you brought here one night to try to interest her.*

SIR TOBY: *Who, Sir Andrew Aguecheek?*

MARIA: *Yes, him.*

SIR TOBY: *He is equal to any man in Illyria.*

MARIA: *How is he equal?*

SIR TOBY: *He makes 3,000 ducats a year.*

MARIA: *Yes, but he will spend them all by the end of the year. He is a fool and a big spender.*

SIR TOBY: *Shame on you for saying that! He plays the violin, speaks three or four languages, and has all of nature's best gifts.*

MARIA: *Indeed, he does, like a born idiot. Moreover, he is not only a fool, he is also argumentative. It is a good thing he has the gift of cowardice to ease his enthusiasm for arguing. If he did not, the wise think he would also have the gift of the grave.*

SIR TOBY: *I swear, the ones who say this about him are scoundrels and slanderers. Who are they?*

MARIA: *They also say he's drunk every night with you.*

SIR TOBY: *He is drunk from drinking to the health of my niece. I will drink to her as long as there is a passage down my throat and alcohol in Illyria. Whoever will not drink to my niece, until his brains spin like a top, is a coward and a lowlife. What, my girl. Speak of the devil. Here comes Sir Andrew Agueface.*

19

[Enter Sir Andrew]

    SIR ANDREW: Sir Toby Belch! how now, Sir Toby Belch!

    SIR TOBY: Sweet Sir Andrew!

40   SIR ANDREW: Bless you, fair shrew.

    MARIA: And you too, sir.

    SIR TOBY: Accost, Sir Andrew, accost.

    SIR ANDREW: What's that?

    SIR TOBY: My niece's chambermaid.

45   SIR ANDREW: Good Mistress Accost, I desire better acquaintance.

    MARIA: My name is Mary, sir.

    SIR ANDREW: Good Mistress Mary Accost,—

    SIR TOBY: You mistake, knight; 'accost' is front her, board her, woo her, assail her.

50   SIR ANDREW: By my troth, I would not undertake her in this company. Is that the meaning of 'accost'?

    MARIA: Fare you well, gentlemen.

    SIR TOBY: An thou let part so, Sir Andrew, would thou mightst never draw sword again.

55   SIR ANDREW: An you part so, mistress, I would I might never draw sword again. Fair lady, do you think you have fools in hand?

    MARIA: Sir, I have not you by the hand.

[Enter Sir Andrew Aguecheek.]

SIR ANDREW: *Sir Toby Belch! How are you, Sir Toby Belch!*

SIR TOBY: *Sweet Sir Andrew!*

SIR ANDREW: *Bless you, pretty vixen.*

MARIA: *And you too, sir.*

SIR TOBY: *Accost her, Sir Andrew. Accost her.*

SIR ANDREW: *What does that mean?*

SIR TOBY: *She is my niece's maid.*

SIR ANDREW: *Dear Mistress Accost, I wish to get to know you better.*

MARIA: *My name is Mary, sir.*

SIR ANDREW: *Dear Mistress Mary Accost—*

SIR TOBY: *You don not understand me, knight. "Accost" means come on to her, approach her, flatter her, attack her.*

SIR ANDREW: *My goodness! I would not attack her in front of you. Is that what "accost" means?*

MARIA: *Goodbye, gentlemen.*

SIR TOBY: *If you let her leave like this, Sir Andrew, you should never draw your sword again.*

SIR ANDREW: *If you leave like this, lady, may I never draw my sword again. Beautiful lady, do you think you have fools on your hands?*

MARIA: *Sir, I am not holding your hand.*

SIR ANDREW: Marry, but you shall have; and here's my hand.

60 MARIA: Now, sir, 'thought is free:' I pray you, bring your hand to the buttery-bar and let it drink.

SIR ANDREW: Wherefore, sweet-heart? what's your metaphor?

MARIA: It's dry, sir.

SIR ANDREW: Why, I think so: I am not such an ass but I can
65 keep my hand dry. But what's your jest?

MARIA: A dry jest, sir.

SIR ANDREW: Are you full of them?

MARIA: Ay, sir, I have them at my fingers' ends: marry, now I let go your hand, I am barren. *[Exit]*

70 SIR TOBY: O knight thou lackest a cup of canary: when did I see thee so put down?

SIR ANDREW: Never in your life, I think; unless you see canary put me down. Methinks sometimes I have no more wit than a Christian or an ordinary man has: but I am a great eater of
75 beef and I believe that does harm to my wit.

SIR TOBY: No question.

SIR ANDREW: An I thought that, I'ld forswear it. I'll ride home tomorrow, Sir Toby.

SIR TOBY: Pourquoi, my dear knight?

80 SIR ANDREW: What is 'Pourquoi'? do or not do? I would I had bestowed that time in the tongues that I have in fencing, dancing and bear-baiting: O, had I but followed the arts!

SIR ANDREW: *Yes, but you will. Here is my hand.*

MARIA: *Well sir, it is free to hope. Bring your hand to the liquor cabinet and let it drink.*

SIR ANDREW: *What do you mean, sweetheart? What are you hinting at?*

MARIA: *Your hand is dry, sir.*

SIR TOBY: *Well, I should hope so. I am not so foolish that I cannot keep my hand dry. However, what is the joke you are making?*

MARIA: *A dry one, sir.*

SIR TOBY: *Are you full of dry jokes?*

MARIA: *Yes, sir. I have them at my fingertips. When I let go of your hand, I will not have any more.* [She exits.]

SIR TOBY: *Oh, knight, you have no wine. When did I see you put it down?*

SIR ANDREW: *I think you have never seen me put a drink down, unless you have seen the wine knock me out. Sometimes I think I have no more intelligence than a Christian or an ordinary man has. However, I eat a lot of beef, and I think that hurts my intelligence.*

SIR TOBY: *Definitely.*

SIR ANDREW: *If I really thought that, I would not eat it anymore. I will go home tomorrow, Sir Toby.*

SIR TOBY: *Porquoi, my dear knight?*

SIR ANDREW: *What is "porquoi"? Do or do not? I wish I had put the time into studying languages that I have put into fencing, dancing, and bear-baiting. Oh, if only I had studied the arts.*

Sir Toby: Then hadst thou had an excellent head of hair.

Sir Andrew: Why, would that have mended my hair?

85   Sir Toby: Past question; for thou seest it will not curl by nature.

Sir Andrew: But it becomes me well enough, does 't not?

Sir Toby: Excellent; it hangs like flax on a distaff; and I hope to
see a housewife take thee between her legs and spin it off.

Sir Andrew: Faith, I'll home to-morrow, Sir Toby: your niece will
90   not be seen; or if she be, it's four to one she'll none of me: the
count himself here hard by woos her.

Sir Toby: She'll none o' the count: she'll not match above her
degree, neither in estate, years, nor wit; I have heard her
swear't. Tut, there's life in't, man.

95   Sir Andrew: I'll stay a month longer. I am a fellow o' the
strangest mind i' the world; I delight in masques and revels
sometimes altogether.

Sir Toby: Art thou good at these kickshawses, knight?

Sir Andrew: As any man in Illyria, whatsoever he be, under the
100   degree of my betters; and yet I will not compare with an old
man.

Sir Toby: What is thy excellence in a galliard, knight?

Sir Andrew: Faith, I can cut a caper.

Sir Toby: And I can cut the mutton to't.

105   Sir Andrew: And I think I have the back-trick simply as strong
as any man in Illyria.

24

SIR TOBY: *Then you would have had an excellent head of hair.*

SIR ANDREW: *Would that have fixed my hair?*

SIR TOBY: *It definitely would have. You see, it will not curl naturally.*

SIR ANDREW: *But it looks good enough, does it not?*

SIR TOBY: *Yes, it looks good on you. It hangs like flax on a spindle. I hope to see a housewife take you between her legs, cut it, and spin it.*

SIR ANDREW: *I will go home tomorrow, Sir Toby. Your niece will not see anyone. Even if she would, I bet she would not see me. The count himself, who lives near here, is pursuing her.*

SIR TOBY: *She does not want anything to do with the count. She will not marry anyone superior to her, whether he has more money, is older, or more intelligent. I have heard her swear to it. You still have a chance, man!*

SIR ANDREW: *I will stay another month. I have the strangest mind in the world. I really enjoy the masquerades and dancing. Sometimes, I like both at the same time.*

SIR TOBY: *Are you good at those types of things?*

SIR ANDREW: *As good as any man in Illyria, as long as he is inferior to me. I am not as good as men with more experience are.*

SIR TOBY: *How good are you at the dance called the galliard, knight?*

SIR ANDREW: *Really, I can cut the caper dance well.*

SIR TOBY: *And I can cut the meat to go with it.*

SIR ANDREW: *I think I do the back-step as well as any man in Illyria.*

SIR TOBY: Wherefore are these things hid? wherefore have these gifts a curtain before 'em? are they like to take dust, like Mistress Mall's picture? why dost thou not go to church in a galliard and come home in a coranto? My very walk should be a jig; I would not so much as make water but in a sink-a-pace. What dost thou mean? Is it a world to hide virtues in? I did think, by the excellent constitution of thy leg, it was formed under the star of a galliard.

110

115 SIR ANDREW: Ay, 'tis strong, and it does indifferent well in a flame-coloured stock. Shall we set about some revels?

SIR TOBY: What shall we do else? were we not born under Taurus?

SIR ANDREW: Taurus! That's sides and heart.

120 SIR TOBY: No, sir; it is legs and thighs. Let me see the caper; ha! higher: ha, ha! excellent!

[Exeunt]

SCENE 4
Duke Orsino's palace.

[Enter Valentine and Viola in man's attire]

VALENTINE: If the duke continue these favours towards you, Cesario, you are like to be much advanced: he hath known you but three days, and already you are no stranger.

VIOLA: You either fear his humour or my negligence, that you call in question the continuance of his love: is he inconstant, sir, in his favours?

5

VALENTINE: No, believe me.

SIR TOBY: *Why do you hide these talents? Why are these gifts concealed with a curtain? Do you think they will collect dust like an old painting? Why don't you go to church doing a galliard and come home doing a different dance? If I were you, my walk would be a jig, and I would not urinate, unless it was in a rhythm. Is this a world to hide your strengths in? I thought, because of the excellent shape of your leg, that it was made under the influence of a dancing star.*

SIR ANDREW: *Yes, it is strong, and it looks good in red colored stockings. Should we do some dancing?*

SIR TOBY: *Of course. Weren't we born under the sign of Taurus?*

SIR ANDREW: *Taurus! That rules the sides and heart.*

SIR TOBY: *No, sir. It rules the legs and thighs. Let me see you dance. Ha! Higher! Ha, ha, that is excellent.*

SCENE 4
The Duke's palace.

[Enter Valentine and Viola, in men's clothing. Viola is now called Cesario]

VALENTINE: *If the Duke keeps favoring you, Cesario, you will probably get a higher position. He has only known you three days and, already, he knows you well.*

VIOLA: *You must be afraid that either he will have a change of heart, or I will neglect him to question if his affection for me will continue. Does he usually keep favoring the same servants?*

VALENTINE: *No, believe me.*

27

VIOLA: I thank you. Here comes the count.

[Enter Duke Orsino, Curio, and Attendants]

DUKE ORSINO: Who saw Cesario, ho?

10   VIOLA: On your attendance, my lord; here.

DUKE ORSINO: Stand you a while aloof, Cesario,
        Thou know'st no less but all; I have unclasp'd
        To thee the book even of my secret soul:
        Therefore, good youth, address thy gait unto her;
15   Be not denied access, stand at her doors,
        And tell them, there thy fixed foot shall grow
        Till thou have audience.

VIOLA: Sure, my noble lord,
        If she be so abandon'd to her sorrow
20   As it is spoke, she never will admit me.

DUKE ORSINO: Be clamorous and leap all civil bounds
        Rather than make unprofited return.

VIOLA: Say I do speak with her, my lord, what then?

DUKE ORSINO: O, then unfold the passion of my love,
25   Surprise her with discourse of my dear faith:
        It shall become thee well to act my woes;
        She will attend it better in thy youth
        Than in a nuncio's of more grave aspect.

VIOLA: I think not so, my lord.

30   DUKE ORSINO: Dear lad, believe it;
        For they shall yet belie thy happy years,
        That say thou art a man: Diana's lip
        Is not more smooth and rubious; thy small pipe
        Is as the maiden's organ, shrill and sound,

VIOLA: *Thank you for telling me. Here comes the count.*

[Enter Duke, Curio, and Attendants.]

DUKE: *Where is Cesario?*

VIOLA: *At your service, my lord. I am here.*

DUKE: *Leave us alone for a while. Cesario, you know everything. I have told you my most secret inner thoughts. Therefore, good boy, go to her. Do not let them keep you out. Stand at her doors, and tell them you will not move until she will listen to you.*

VIOLA: *My noble lord, surely if she is as absorbed by her sorrow as people say, she will never let me in.*

DUKE: *You should make a scene and act rudely rather than come back here without having spoken to her.*

VIOLA: *If I do speak to her, my lord, what should I say?*

DUKE: *Tell her about the passion of my love. Surprise her by talking about my devotedness to her. It will be appropriate for you to also describe to her my sorrows. She will listen to it better coming from a young person than from an older messenger.*

VIOLA: *I do not think so, my lord.*

DUKE: *Dear boy, believe it. They would be denying you the happy years of growing up, if they call you a man. Your lips are as smooth and red as Diana's. Your small windpipe is like a young woman's voice, high-pitched and steady. All of these features are like a woman's. I know you are the right one to do this task.* [To Attendants] *Send four or five men*

35 And all is semblative a woman's part.
I know thy constellation is right apt
For this affair. Some four or five attend him;
All, if you will; for I myself am best
When least in company. Prosper well in this,
40 And thou shalt live as freely as thy lord,
To call his fortunes thine.

VIOLA: I'll do my best
To woo your lady: [Aside] yet, a barful strife!
Whoe'er I woo, myself would be his wife.

[Exeunt]

SCENE 5
Olivia's house.

[Enter Maria and Clown]

MARIA: Nay, either tell me where thou hast been, or I will not
open my lips so wide as a bristle may enter in way of thy
excuse: my lady will hang thee for thy absence.

CLOWN: Let her hang me: he that is well hanged in this world
5 needs to fear no colours.

MARIA: Make that good.

CLOWN: He shall see none to fear.

MARIA: A good lenten answer: I can tell thee where that saying
was born, of 'I fear no colours.'

10 CLOWN: Where, good Mistress Mary?

with him. All of you can go if you want. I am better off with fewer people around. Do this well, and you shall live as comfortably as your lord you will and call my fortune your own.

VIOLA: *I will do my best to win over your lady.* [Aside] *However, it will be difficult, because no matter whom I pursue for him, I myself would like to be his wife.*

[They exit.]

SCENE 5
Olivia's house.

[Enter Maria and Feste, a Clown.]

MARIA: *No, either tell me where you have been, or I will not open my mouth as wide as a hair to make excuses for you. My lady will hang you for your absence.*

CLOWN: *Let her hang me. He that is well hanged in this world does not need to fear the colors.*

MARIA: *What does that mean?*

CLOWN: *He will not be able to see any thing to fear.*

MARIA: *That is a good simple answer. I can tell you where that saying, "I fear no colors," comes from.*

CLOWN: *Where, good Mistress Mary?*

MARIA: In the wars; and that may you be bold to say in your
foolery.

CLOWN: Well, God give them wisdom that have it; and those that
are fools, let them use their talents.

15 MARIA: Yet you will be hanged for being so long absent; or, to be
turned away, is not that as good as a hanging to you?

CLOWN: Many a good hanging prevents a bad marriage; and, for
turning away, let summer bear it out.

MARIA: You are resolute, then?

20 CLOWN: Not so, neither; but I am resolved on two points.

MARIA: That if one break, the other will hold; or, if both break,
your gaskins fall.

CLOWN: Apt, in good faith; very apt. Well, go thy way; if Sir Toby
would leave drinking, thou wert as witty a piece of Eve's flesh
25 as any in Illyria.

MARIA: Peace, you rogue, no more o' that. Here comes my lady:
make your excuse wisely, you were best.   *[Exit]*

CLOWN: Wit, an't be thy will, put me into good fooling! Those
wits, that think they have thee, do very oft prove fools; and I,
30 that am sure I lack thee, may pass for a wise man: for what
says Quinapalus? 'Better a witty fool, than a foolish wit.'

[Enter Olivia with Malvolio]
God bless thee, lady!

OLIVIA: Take the fool away.

CLOWN: Do you not hear, fellows? Take away the lady.

MARIA: *During the wars. Now you can be comfortable using it in your foolish jokes.*

CLOWN: *Well, God gives wisdom to the wise. Let those who are fools use their talent.*

MARIA: *Still, my lady will have you hanged for being gone so long, or she will send you away. Isn't that the same as hanging for you?*

CLOWN: *Many good hangings prevent bad marriages. As for being fired, let us wait and see what happens.*

MARIA: *You are persistent then?*

CLOWN: *No, but I am firm on two points.*

MARIA: *If one breaks, the other will hold, or, if both break, your pants will fall down?*

CLOWN: *Well done, honestly, well done. Well, go on your way. If Sir Toby would stop drinking, you would be as witty a woman as any in Illyria.*

MARIA: *Stop, you rascal, that is enough. Here comes my lady. You had better make a good excuse.*   [Exit]

CLOWN: *Wit, if it is your will, do your best! Clowns that think they are witty usually turn out to be fools. Since I know I am not witty, I may pass for a wise man. What does Quinapalus say? "Better a witty fool than a foolish wit."*

[Enter Lady Olivia with Malvolio.]
   God bless you, lady!

OLIVIA: *Take the fool away.*

CLOWN: *Didn't you hear, men? Take the lady away.*

35   OLIVIA: Go to, you're a dry fool; I'll no more of you: besides, you
grow dishonest.

CLOWN: Two faults, madonna, that drink and good counsel will
amend: for give the dry fool drink, then is the fool not dry:
bid the dishonest man mend himself; if he mend, he is no
40   longer dishonest; if he cannot, let the botcher mend him.
Any thing that's mended is but patched: virtue that
transgresses is but patched with sin; and sin that amends is
but patched with virtue. If that this simple syllogism will
serve, so; if it will not, what remedy? As there is no true
45   cuckold but calamity, so beauty's a flower. The lady bade
take away the fool; therefore, I say again, take her away.

OLIVIA: Sir, I bade them take away you.

CLOWN: Misprision in the highest degree! Lady, cucullus non
facit monachum; that's as much to say as I wear not motley
50   in my brain. Good madonna, give me leave to prove you a
fool.

OLIVIA: Can you do it?

CLOWN: Dexterously, good madonna.

OLIVIA: Make your proof.

55   CLOWN: I must catechise you for it, madonna: good my mouse of
virtue, answer me.

OLIVIA: Well, sir, for want of other idleness, I'll bide your proof.

CLOWN: Good madonna, why mournest thou?

OLIVIA: Good fool, for my brother's death.

60   CLOWN: I think his soul is in hell, madonna.

34

OLIVIA: *Stop your nonsense. You have a dry wit. I am sick of you. Besides, you have become dishonest.*

CLOWN: *Two faults, my lady, which alcohol and good advice will fix. If you give the dry fool a drink, then the fool is not dry. Ask the dishonest man to mend himself, and, if he does, he is no longer dishonest. If he cannot mend himself, then let the tailor mend him. Anything that is mended is only patched up. Virtue that slips up is only patched with sin. A sin that is fixed is only patched with virtue. If this logical reasoning is pleasing to you, good. If it is not, how can I fix it? There is no true way to learn, except by misfortune. Like a flower, beauty fades. The lady ordered you to take the fool away. So, I say again, take her away.*

OLIVIA: *Sir, I ordered them to take you away.*

CLOWN: *You mock me terribly! Lady, the hood does not make the monk. That means I am dressed as a fool, but my mind does not wear fool's clothing. Good lady, give me permission to prove that you are the fool.*

OLIVIA: *Can you do it?*

CLOWN: *Skillfully, good lady.*

OLIVIA: *Prove it.*

CLOWN: *I must question you to do it, lady. My good, virtuous mouse must answer me.*

OLIVIA: *Well, sir, for lack of anything better to do, I will hear your proof.*

CLOWN: *Good lady, why do you mourn?*

OLIVIA: *Good fool, for my brother's death.*

CLOWN: *I think his soul is in hell, lady.*

OLIVIA: I know his soul is in heaven, fool.

CLOWN: The more fool, madonna, to mourn for your brother's
soul being in heaven. Take away the fool, gentlemen.

OLIVIA: What think you of this fool, Malvolio? doth he not
65   mend?

MALVOLIO: Yes, and shall do till the pangs of death shake him:
infirmity, that decays the wise, doth ever make the better
fool.

CLOWN: God send you, sir, a speedy infirmity, for the better
70   increasing your folly! Sir Toby will be sworn that I am no
fox; but he will not pass his word for two pence that you are
no fool.

OLIVIA: How say you to that, Malvolio?

MALVOLIO: I marvel your ladyship takes delight in such a barren
75   rascal: I saw him put down the other day with an ordinary
fool that has no more brain than a stone. Look you now, he's
out of his guard already; unless you laugh and minister
occasion to him, he is gagged. I protest, I take these wise
men, that crow so at these set kind of fools, no better than
80   the fools' zanies.

OLIVIA: Oh, you are sick of self-love, Malvolio, and taste with a
distempered appetite. To be generous, guiltless and of free
disposition, is to take those things for bird-bolts that you
deem cannon-bullets: there is no slander in an allowed fool,
85   though he do nothing but rail; nor no railing in a known
discreet man, though he do nothing but reprove.

CLOWN: Now Mercury endue thee with leasing, for thou speakest
well of fools!

[Re-enter Maria]

OLIVIA: I know his soul is in heaven, fool.

CLOWN: You are more of a fool, lady, to mourn because your brother's soul is in heaven. Take away the fool, gentlemen.

OLIVIA: What do you think of this fool, Malvolio? Doesn't he redeem himself?

MALVOLIO: Yes, and he will continue to until he lies dying. Old age that impairs wise men, improves the fool.

CLOWN: God send you, sir, a speedy old age, so it will increase you foolishness even more! Sir Toby will swear that I am not a clever man, but he will not swear for two pennies that you are not a fool.

OLIVIA: What do you say to that, Malvolio?

MALVOLIO: I am amazed that you enjoy such a stupid rascal. I saw him put to silence the other day by an ordinary fool that has no more brains than a stone. Look at him now. He is unstable already. Unless you laugh and urge him on, he falls silent. I swear, I think the wise men that laugh so loudly at these kinds of fools are no better than the buffoons that mimic the clowns.

OLIVIA: Oh, you are too full of yourself, Malvolio. It makes your perceptions bitter and prejudiced. If you want to be generous, innocent, and kind, you must take as arrows the things you are calling cannon balls. There is nothing wrong with a fool, even if he does nothing but rave. Nor is there anything wrong with raving from a respectable man, even if he does nothing but disapprove.

CLOWN: May Mercury grant you the gift of lying for speaking well of fools!

[Re-enter Maria.]

MARIA: Madam, there is at the gate a young gentleman much
90   desires to speak with you.

OLIVIA: From the Count Orsino, is it?

MARIA: I know not, madam: 'tis a fair young man, and well
attended.

OLIVIA: Who of my people hold him in delay?

95   MARIA: Sir Toby, madam, your kinsman.

OLIVIA: Fetch him off, I pray you; he speaks nothing but mad
man: fie on him!   *[Exit Maria]*
Go you, Malvolio: if it be a suit from the count, I am sick, or
not at home; what you will, to dismiss it. *[Exit Malvolio]*
100   Now you see, sir, how your fooling grows old, and people
dislike it.

CLOWN: Thou hast spoke for us, madonna, as if thy eldest son
should be a fool; whose skull Jove cram with brains! for,—
here he comes,—one of thy kin has a most weak pia mater.

[Enter Sir Toby]

105   OLIVIA: By mine honour, half drunk. What is he at the gate,
cousin?

SIR TOBY: A gentleman.

OLIVIA: A gentleman! what gentleman?

SIR TOBY: 'Tis a gentle man here—a plague o' these pickle-her-
110   ring! How now, sot!

CLOWN: Good Sir Toby!

MARIA: *Madam, there is a young man at your gate who greatly desires to speak with you.*

OLIVIA: *Did Count Orsino send him?*

MARIA: *I do not know, madam. He is an attractive young man and accompanied by many servants.*

OLIVIA: *Who is stopping him from coming in?*

MARIA: *Your uncle, Sir Toby, madam.*

OLIVIA: *Please get him away from there. Shame on him. He talks like a madman!* [Exit Maria.] *Malvolio, go to the young man. If he was sent to flatter me by the count, say I am sick, or not at home. Say what ever you need to in order to make him leave.* [Exit Malvolio.] *Now you see, sir, how your joking becomes tiresome, and people do not like it.*

CLOWN: *You have spoken about fools, lady, as if your oldest son is a fool. May God fill his skull with brains! Here comes one of your relatives who does not have enough of them.*

[Enter Sir Toby.]

OLIVIA: *I swear, he is half drunk. Who is at the gate, uncle?*

SIR TOBY: *A gentleman.*

OLIVIA: *A gentleman! What gentleman?*

SIR TOBY: *There is a gentleman here. Curse these pickled-herrings! Hello, fool!*

CLOWN: *Good Sir Toby!*

OLIVIA: Cousin, cousin, how have you come so early by this lethargy?

SIR TOBY: Lechery! I defy lechery. There's one at the gate.

115 OLIVIA: Ay, marry, what is he?

SIR TOBY: Let him be the devil, an he will, I care not: give me faith, say I. Well, it's all one. *[Exit]*

OLIVIA: What's a drunken man like, fool?

CLOWN: Like a drowned man, a fool and a mad man: one
120 draught above heat makes him a fool; the second mads him; and a third drowns him.

OLIVIA: Go thou and seek the crowner, and let him sit o' my coz; for he's in the third degree of drink, he's drowned: go, look after him.

125 CLOWN: He is but mad yet, madonna; and the fool shall look to the madman. *[Exit]*

[Re-enter Malvolio]

MALVOLIO: Madam, yond young fellow swears he will speak with you. I told him you were sick; he takes on him to understand so much, and therefore comes to speak with you. I told him
130 you were asleep; he seems to have a foreknowledge of that too, and therefore comes to speak with you. What is to be said to him, lady? he's fortified against any denial.

OLIVIA: Tell him he shall not speak with me.

MALVOLIO: Has been told so; and he says, he'll stand at your door
135 like a sheriff's post, and be the supporter to a bench, but he'll speak with you.

OLIVIA: *Uncle, uncle, how have you come upon this lethargy so early?*

SIR TOBY: *Lechery! I hate lechery. There is some one at the gate.*

OLIVIA: *Oh, for goodness sake, who is he?*

SIR TOBY: *He might as well be the devil. I do not care. Give me God, I say. Well, it is all the same thing.*   [He exits.]

OLIVIA: *What is a drunken man like, fool?*

CLOWN: *He is like a man who has drowned, a fool, and a madman. One drink too many makes him a fool. The second makes him crazy, and the third drowns him.*

OLIVIA: *Go find the coroner, and let him sit with my uncle, because he is at the third degree of drunk. He is drowned. Go take care of him.*

CLOWN: *So far, he is only crazy, madam. I will go take care of the mad-man.*

                                              [Exit.]

[Re-enter Malvolio.]

MALVOLIO: *Madam, that young man swears he must speak with you. I told him you were sick. He claimed he knew that, and, therefore, had come to speak with you. I told him you were asleep. He seemed to know that too, and, therefore, also wants to speak with you. What should I say to him, lady? He will not accept any excuses.*

OLIVIA: *Tell him he cannot speak with me.*

MALVOLIO: *I have already told him that. He says he will stand at your door like a pole, or hold up a bench, but he will stay until he speaks with you.*

OLIVIA: What kind o' man is he?

MALVOLIO: Why, of mankind.

OLIVIA: What manner of man?

140 MALVOLIO: Of very ill manner; he'll speak with you, will you or no.

OLIVIA: Of what personage and years is he?

MALVOLIO: Not yet old enough for a man, nor young enough for a boy; as a squash is before 'tis a peascod, or a cooling when
145 'tis almost an apple: 'tis with him in standing water, between boy and man. He is very well-favoured and he speaks very shrewishly; one would think his mother's milk were scarce out of him.

OLIVIA: Let him approach: call in my gentlewoman.

150 MALVOLIO: Gentlewoman, my lady calls.   *[Exit]*

[Re-enter Maria]

OLIVIA: Give me my veil: come, throw it o'er my face. We'll once more hear Orsino's embassy.

[Enter Viola, and Attendants]

VIOLA: The honourable lady of the house, which is she?

OLIVIA: Speak to me; I shall answer for her. Your will?

155 VIOLA: Most radiant, exquisite and unmatchable beauty,—I pray you, tell me if this be the lady of the house, for I never saw her: I would be loath to cast away my speech, for besides that it is excellently well penned, I have taken great pains to con it. Good beauties, let me sustain no scorn; I am very
160 comptible, even to the least sinister usage.

OLIVIA: *What kind of man is he?*

MALVOLIO: *A human.*

OLIVIA: *What sort of man?*

MALVOLIO: *A very disagreeable sort of man. He will speak with you whether you want to or not.*

OLIVIA: *What does he look like, and how old is he?*

MALVOLIO: *He is not old enough to be called a man, but not young enough to be a boy. He is like an unripe pea or a developing apple. He is standing in the still water between being a boy and a man. He is very attractive and speaks shrilly, like a woman. One would think he had only just stopped drinking his mother's milk.*

OLIVIA: *Let him come talk to me. Call in my maid.*

MALVOLIO: *Maid, my lady needs you.*

[Re-enter Maria.]

OLIVIA: *Give me my veil. Come here, and throw it over my face. We will again hear Orsino's message.*

[Enter Viola, and Attendants.]

VIOLA: *The honorable lady of the house, who is she?*

OLIVIA: *Speak to me. I will answer for her. What do you want?*

VIOLA: *Most radiant, exquisite and unmatchable beauty...Please tell me if this is the lady of the house, because I have never seen her. It would be terrible to waste my speech, because, not only is it well written, but I have also worked hard to memorize it. Good ladies, please do not make fun of me. I am very sensitive, even to the slightest mistreatment.*

OLIVIA: Whence came you, sir?

VIOLA: I can say little more than I have studied, and that
    question's out of my part. Good gentle one, give me modest
    assurance if you be the lady of the house, that I may proceed
165   in my speech.

OLIVIA: Are you a comedian?

VIOLA: No, my profound heart: and yet, by the very fangs of
    malice I swear, I am not that I play. Are you the lady of the
    house?

170   OLIVIA: If I do not usurp myself, I am.

VIOLA: Most certain, if you are she, you do usurp yourself; for
    what is yours to bestow is not yours to reserve. But this is
    from my commission: I will on with my speech in your
    praise, and then show you the heart of my message.

175   OLIVIA: Come to what is important in't: I forgive you the praise.

VIOLA: Alas, I took great pains to study it, and 'tis poetical.

OLIVIA: It is the more like to be feigned: I pray you, keep it in. I
    heard you were saucy at my gates, and allowed your
    approach rather to wonder at you than to hear you. If you be
180   not mad, be gone; if you have reason, be brief: 'tis not that
    time of moon with me to make one in so skipping a dialogue.

MARIA: Will you hoist sail, sir? here lies your way.

VIOLA: No, good swabber; I am to hull here a little longer. Some
    mollification for your giant, sweet lady. Tell me your mind: I
185   am a messenger.

OLIVIA: Sure, you have some hideous matter to deliver, when the
    courtesy of it is so fearful. Speak your office.

OLIVIA: *Where have you come from, sir?*

VIOLA: *I cannot say much more than what I have prepared, and that question is not part of my speech. Good lady, give me some assurance that you are the lady of the house, so that I can go on with my speech.*

OLIVIA: *Are you an actor?*

VIOLA: *No, bless me, but I swear, despite terrible rumors, I am not what I seem to be. Are you the lady of the house?*

OLIVIA: *Unless I do myself a wrong, I am.*

VIOLA: *Surely, if you are she, you are doing yourself a wrong, because what is yours to give away is not yours to keep. However, this is coming from me personally. I will go on with my speech in praise of you and then show you the point of my message.*

OLIVIA: *Get to the important part. I will excuse you from giving the praise.*

VIOLA: *Oh, but I have worked very hard to learn it, and it is poetic.*

OLIVIA: *It is likely to be insincere. Please, do not say it. I heard you were rude at my gates, and I let you in more to have you entertain me than to listen to you. If you are crazy, go away. If you are sane, be brief. I am in no mood to have this silly conversation with you.*

MARIA: *Are you going to sail out of here, sir? Here is your path.*

VIOLA: *No, good deck-mopper. I am going to drift here a little longer. Please calm down your giant, sweet lady. Tell me what you think. I am a messenger.*

OLIVIA: *Surely, you must have some terrible news to deliver, when the presentation of it is so alarming. Deliver your message.*

VIOLA: It alone concerns your ear. I bring no overture of war, no
taxation of homage: I hold the olive in my hand; my words
190   are as fun of peace as matter.

OLIVIA: Yet you began rudely. What are you? what would you?

VIOLA: The rudeness that hath appeared in me have I learned
from my entertainment. What I am, and what I would, are as
secret as maidenhead; to your ears, divinity, to any other's,
195   profanation.

OLIVIA: Give us the place alone: we will hear this divinity.
               [Exeunt Maria and Attendants]
Now, sir, what is your text?

VIOLA: Most sweet lady,—

OLIVIA: A comfortable doctrine, and much may be said of it.
200   Where lies your text?

VIOLA: In Orsino's bosom.

OLIVIA: In his bosom! In what chapter of his bosom?

VIOLA: To answer by the method, in the first of his heart.

OLIVIA: O, I have read it: it is heresy. Have you no more to say?

205 VIOLA: Good madam, let me see your face.

OLIVIA: Have you any commission from your lord to negotiate
with my face? You are now out of your text: but we will draw
the curtain and show you the picture. Look you, sir, such a
one I was this present: is 't not well done?
                      [Unveiling]

210 VIOLA: Excellently done, if God did all.

VIOLA: *You are the only one who needs to hear it. I bring no news of war, no demand for money to pay your allegiance. I come in peace. My words are peaceful.*

OLIVIA: *But you began rudely. Who are you? What do you want?*

VIOLA: *My rudeness came in response to how I was treated at the gate. Who I am and what I want are as secret as virginity. To your ears, what I have to say will be divine. To anyone else's profane.*

OLIVIA: *Leave us alone in this room. I will hear this divinity.*
[Exit Maria and Attendants.]
Now, sir, what do you have to say?

VIOLA: *Most sweet lady, —*

OLIVIA: *A safe, biblical way to begin, and a lot may be said for it. Where does your theme come from?*

VIOLA: *From Orsino's heart.*

OLIVIA: *From his heart! From what part of his heart?*

VIOLA: *To answer on your terms, Chapter One of his heart.*

OLIVIA: *Oh, I have read it. It is blasphemous. Don't you have anything else to say?*

VIOLA: *Good madam, let me see your face.*

OLIVIA: *Has your lord given you authority to negotiate with my face? You are not going by your script. However, I will pull back the veil and show you the picture. Look at it, sir, this is how I looked just now. Isn't it well done?*

VIOLA: *It is excellently done, if God made it all.*

OLIVIA: 'Tis in grain, sir; 'twill endure wind and weather.

VIOLA: 'Tis beauty truly blent, whose red and white
    Nature's own sweet and cunning hand laid on:
    Lady, you are the cruell'st she alive,
215   If you will lead these graces to the grave
    And leave the world no copy.

OLIVIA: O, sir, I will not be so hard-hearted; I will give out divers
    schedules of my beauty: it shall be inventoried, and every
    particle and utensil labelled to my will: as, item, two lips,
220   indifferent red; item, two grey eyes, with lids to them; item,
    one neck, one chin, and so forth. Were you sent hither to
    praise me?

VIOLA: I see you what you are, you are too proud;
    But, if you were the devil, you are fair.
225   My lord and master loves you: O, such love
    Could be but recompensed, though you were crown'd
    The nonpareil of beauty!

OLIVIA: How does he love me?

VIOLA: With adorations, fertile tears,
230   With groans that thunder love, with sighs of fire.

OLIVIA: Your lord does know my mind; I cannot love him:
    Yet I suppose him virtuous, know him noble,
    Of great estate, of fresh and stainless youth;
    In voices well divulged, free, learn'd and valiant;
235   And in dimension and the shape of nature
    A gracious person: but yet I cannot love him;
    He might have took his answer long ago.

VIOLA: If I did love you in my master's flame,
    With such a suffering, such a deadly life,
240   In your denial I would find no sense;
    I would not understand it.

OLIVIA: It is permanent, sir. It will endure the wind and weather.

VIOLA: Your beauty is blended well. Nature's sweet and skillful hand applied the reds and whites. Lady, you are the cruelest woman alive if you will take your beauty to the grave and not leave the world a copy.

OLIVIA: Oh, sir, I will not be that cruel. I will give out several itemized lists of my beauty. It will be inventoried, and every detail and tool will be labeled with whom I wish to leave it to. For instance: item: two lips, fairly red; item, two gray eyes with lids; item, one neck, one chin, and so on. Were you sent here to appraise me?

VIOLA: I see you for what you are. You are too proud. However, even if you are the devil, you are beautiful. My lord and master loves you. Oh, and such love could only be repaid if you were named the most beautiful woman in the world.

OLIVIA: How does he love me?

VIOLA: With words of adoration, flowing tears, great groans of love, and passionate sighs.

OLIVIA: Your lord already knows what I think. I cannot love him. Nevertheless, I assume that he is respectable. I know that he is noble, wealthy, and an uncorrupted young man. Everyone speaks of him well. He is worthy, intelligent, and valiant. He is an attractive person. However, I cannot love him. He should have accepted my answer a long time ago.

VIOLA: If I loved you as intensely as my master, with so much suffering and such a death-like existence, I would not be able to find sense in your denial. I would not understand it.

OLIVIA: Why, what would you?

VIOLA: Make me a willow cabin at your gate,
  And call upon my soul within the house;
245   Write loyal cantons of contemned love
  And sing them loud even in the dead of night;
  Halloo your name to the reverberate hills
  And make the babbling gossip of the air
  Cry out 'Olivia!' O, You should not rest
250   Between the elements of air and earth,
  But you should pity me!

OLIVIA: You might do much.
  What is your parentage?

VIOLA: Above my fortunes, yet my state is well:
255   I am a gentleman.

OLIVIA: Get you to your lord;
  I cannot love him: let him send no more;
  Unless, perchance, you come to me again,
  To tell me how he takes it. Fare you well:
260   I thank you for your pains: spend this for me.

VIOLA: I am no fee'd post, lady; keep your purse:
  My master, not myself, lacks recompense.
  Love make his heart of flint that you shall love;
  And let your fervor, like my master's, be
265   Placed in contempt! Farewell, fair cruelty.   *[Exit]*

OLIVIA: 'What is your parentage?'
  'Above my fortunes, yet my state is well:
  I am a gentleman.' I'll be sworn thou art;
  Thy tongue, thy face, thy limbs, actions and spirit,
270   Do give thee five-fold blazon: not too fast: soft, soft!
  Unless the master were the man. How now!
  Even so quickly may one catch the plague?
  Methinks I feel this youth's perfections

OLIVIA: *What would you do?*

VIOLA: *I would live under the willow tree by your gate, and call out to my loved one inside the house. I would write genuine songs of forlorn love and sing them loudly, even in the middle of the night. I would yell your name out to the echoing hills and have the air call back, "Olivia!" Oh, you would not be able to live without pitying me.*

OLIVIA: *You might succeed if you did that. What is your rank?*

VIOLA: *Above my present position, but my background is respectable. I am a gentleman.*

OLIVIA: *Go back to your lord. Tell him I cannot love him and not to send anyone else. Unless, perhaps, you come back to tell me how he took the news. Goodbye. Thank you for your trouble, and take this money.*

VIOLA: *I am not a hired messenger, lady. Keep your money. My master, not I, needs compensation. May the heart of the one you love be made of stone. Let your dedication, like my masters, be scorned. Goodbye, beautiful, cruel woman.* [Exit.]

OLIVIA: *"What is your rank?" "Above my present position, but my background is respectable. I am a gentleman." I will swear to it that you are. Your voice, your face, your limbs, actions, and personality indicate that you are of high rank. Not too fast; slow down. I wish the master were the messenger. What is this! Can I fall in love this fast? I think this young man's perfection is sneakily and unnoticeably creeping in through my eyes. So be it. Hello, Malvolio!*

With an invisible and subtle stealth
275   To creep in at mine eyes. Well, let it be.
What ho, Malvolio!

[Re-enter Malvolio]

MALVOLIO: Here, madam, at your service.

OLIVIA: Run after that same peevish messenger,
The county's man: he left this ring behind him,
280   Would I or not: tell him I'll none of it.
Desire him not to flatter with his lord,
Nor hold him up with hopes; I am not for him:
If that the youth will come this way to-morrow,
I'll give him reasons for't: hie thee, Malvolio.

285 MALVOLIO: Madam, I will.   *[Exit]*

OLIVIA: I do I know not what, and fear to find
Mine eye too great a flatterer for my mind.
Fate, show thy force: ourselves we do not owe;
What is decreed must be, and be this so.

                      [Exit]

[Re-enter Malvolio.]

MALVOLIO: *I am here, madam, at your service.*

OLIVIA: *Run after that obstinate messenger, the count's man. He left this ring here, whether I wanted it or not. Tell him I do not want it. Tell him to be straightforward with his master and not give him false hope. I am not the woman for him. If that young man comes back tomorrow, I will tell him why. Quickly, Malvolio.*

MALVOLIO: *Madam, I will.* [He exits.]

OLIVIA: *I do not know what I am doing and am afraid that my eyes are deceiving my mind. Fate, show your power. We are not in control of our lives. What is meant to be must be, and this will not be any different.*

[She exits.]

ACT II

SCENE 1
The sea-coast.

[Enter Antonio and Sebastian]

ANTONIO: Will you stay no longer? nor will you not that I go
    with you?

SEBASTIAN: By your patience, no. My stars shine darkly over me:
    the malignancy of my fate might perhaps distemper yours;
5   therefore I shall crave of you your leave that I may bear my
    evils alone: it were a bad recompense for your love, to
    lay any of them on you.

ANTONIO: Let me yet know of you whither you are bound.

SEBASTIAN: No, sooth, sir: my determinate voyage is mere
10   extravagancy. But I perceive in you so excellent a touch of
    modesty, that you will not extort from me what I am willing
    to keep in; therefore it charges me in manners the rather to
    express myself. You must know of me then, Antonio, my
    name is Sebastian, which I called Roderigo. My father was
15   that Sebastian of Messaline, whom I know you have heard of.
    He left behind him myself and a sister, both born in an hour:
    if the heavens had been pleased, would we had so ended! but
    you, sir, altered that; for some hour before you took me from
    the breach of the sea was my sister drowned.

20   ANTONIO: Alas the day!

ACT II

SCENE 1
The sea-coast.

[Enter Antonio and Sebastian.]

ANTONIO: *Won't you stay any longer or let me go with you?*

SEBASTIAN: *I am sorry, but no. My poor fortune hangs over me, and my bad luck might harm your fate. Therefore, I want you to leave me to deal with my misfortune alone. It would not be a just payment for your friendship to burden you with my situation.*

ANTONIO: *Please let me know where you are going.*

SEBASTIAN: *No, truly, sir. The voyage I am going on has no set destination. However, I can tell by your politeness that you will not try to find out what I would rather not tell you. Therefore, out of good manners, I will tell you what I can. You must have heard of me, Antonio; my name is Sebastian, although I told you to call me Roderigo. My father was Sebastian of Messaline. I know you have heard of him. When he died, he left behind my sister and me. We were born during the same hour, and, if the heavens would have had their way, we would have died during the same hour! However, you, sir, changed that, because about an hour before you saved me from the waves of the sea, my sister drowned.*

ANTONIO: *That is terrible!*

SEBASTIAN: A lady, sir, though it was said she much resembled
me, was yet of many accounted beautiful: but, though I could
not with such estimable wonder overfar believe that, yet thus
far I will boldly publish her; she bore a mind that envy could
25   not but call fair. She is drowned already, sir, with salt water,
though I seem to drown her remembrance again with more.

ANTONIO: Pardon me, sir, your bad entertainment.

SEBASTIAN: O good Antonio, forgive me your trouble.

ANTONIO: If you will not murder me for my love, let me be
30   your servant.

SEBASTIAN: If you will not undo what you have done, that is,
kill him whom you have recovered, desire it not. Fare ye well
at once: my bosom is full of kindness, and I am yet so near
the manners of my mother, that upon the least occasion more
35   mine eyes will tell tales of me. I am bound to the Count
Orsino's court: farewell.   [Exit]

ANTONIO: The gentleness of all the gods go with thee!
I have many enemies in Orsino's court,
Else would I very shortly see thee there.
40   But, come what may, I do adore thee so,
That danger shall seem sport, and I will go.   [Exit]

SEBASTIAN: *Although people said she looked a lot like me, she was thought to be a beautiful lady, sir. Even though I cannot exaggerate and say I believed that, I will boldly talk about her other qualities. She had a mind that not even an envious person could deny was excellent. She is drowned in the salt water already, sir, and I seem to drown her memories with even more.*

ANTONIO: *Please excuse my unworthy treatment of you, sir.*

SEBASTIAN: *Oh, good Antonio, forgive me for being so much trouble.*

ANTONIO: *If you do not want me to die from wanting to be with you, let me be your servant.*

SEBASTIAN: *If you do not want to undo what you have done, that is kill me, who you have just saved, do not ask to serve me. Leave me now. My heart is so full of affection for you, and I am so much like my mother, that for any further talk, my eyes will betray my true feelings. I am going to the Count Orsino's court. Goodbye.* [He exits.]

ANTONIO: *May the protection of all the gods follow you! I have many enemies in Orsino's court, or else I would follow you there. However, no matter what happens, I care so much for you that I will face that danger as if it were a game. I will follow you.* [He exits.]

SCENE 2
A street.

[Enter Viola, Malvolio following]

MALVOLIO: Were not you even now with the Countess Olivia?

VIOLA: Even now, sir; on a moderate pace I have since arrived
    but hither.

MALVOLIO: She returns this ring to you, sir: you might have saved
5   me my pains, to have taken it away yourself. She adds,
    moreover, that you should put your lord into a desperate
    assurance she will none of him: and one thing more, that you
    be never so hardy to come again in his affairs, unless it be to
    report your lord's taking of this. Receive it so.

10   VIOLA: She took the ring of me: I'll none of it.

MALVOLIO: Come, sir, you peevishly threw it to her; and her will
    is, it should be so returned: if it be worth stooping for, there
    it lies in your eye; if not, be it his that finds it.   *[Exit]*

VIOLA: I left no ring with her: what means this lady?
15   Fortune forbid my outside have not charm'd her!
    She made good view of me; indeed, so much,
    That sure methought her eyes had lost her tongue,
    For she did speak in starts distractedly.
    She loves me, sure; the cunning of her passion
20   Invites me in this churlish messenger.
    None of my lord's ring! why, he sent her none.
    I am the man: if it be so, as 'tis,
    Poor lady, she were better love a dream.
    Disguise, I see, thou art a wickedness,
25   Wherein the pregnant enemy does much.
    How easy is it for the proper-false
    In women's waxen hearts to set their forms!

SCENE 2
A street.

[Enter Viola with Malvolio following.]

MALVOLIO: *Weren't you just with the Countess Olivia?*

VIOLA: *I was just there, sir. Walking slowly, I have just arrived at this spot.*

MALVOLIO: *She is giving this ring back to you, sir. You would have saved me the trouble by taking it away yourself. She also says that you should inform your lord that she will not have anything to do with him. One more thing: do not ever visit and brazenly proclaim the duke's love again, unless you come back to tell her how your lord takes this news. Here is the ring.*

VIOLA: *She took the ring from me. I will not take it back.*

MALVOLIO: *Oh, come on, sir. You stubbornly threw it at her, and she wants to return it in the same way. If it is worth stooping down to pick it up, there it is, where you can see it. If it is not, let whoever finds it keep it.*

[He exits.]

VIOLA: *I did not leave a ring with her. Why is she doing this? Heaven forbid that she is attracted to me! She looked me over well. Indeed, so well that I thought her eyes had made her lose her train of thought, because she spoke in stops and starts, disjointedly. She loves me for sure. It is cleverness, created by her passion for me, which made her invite me back as a rude messenger. She will not have my lord's ring! Well, he did not send her one. I am the man she wants. If that is true, the poor lady, she would be better off loving a dream. Disguise, I see, you are wicked, allowing the devil to do his will. How easy it is for a philanderer to make a lady set her heart on him. Unfortunately, our weakness to temptation is at fault, not us! Because what we are made of is what we will be. How will this turn out? My master loves her dearly, and I, poor monster, love him just as much. Finally, she, mistakenly, seems to love me. How will this end? As a man, it is hopeless that I might win my master's love. As*

Alas, our frailty is the cause, not we!
For such as we are made of, such we be.
30   How will this fadge? my master loves her dearly;
And I, poor monster, fond as much on him;
And she, mistaken, seems to dote on me.
What will become of this? As I am man,
My state is desperate for my master's love;
35   As I am woman,—now alas the day!—
What thriftless sighs shall poor Olivia breathe!
O time! thou must untangle this, not I;
It is too hard a knot for me to untie!   [Exit]

SCENE 3
Olivia's house.

[Enter Sir Toby and Sir Andrew]

SIR TOBY: Approach, Sir Andrew: not to be abed after midnight
is to be up betimes; and 'diluculo surgere,' thou know'st,—

SIR ANDREW: Nay, my troth, I know not: but I know, to be up
late is to be up late.

5   SIR TOBY: A false conclusion: I hate it as an unfilled can. To be
up after midnight and to go to bed then, is early: so that to
go to bed after midnight is to go to bed betimes. Does not
our life consist of the four elements?

SIR ANDREW: Faith, so they say; but I think it rather consists of
10   eating and drinking.

SIR TOBY: Thou 'rt a scholar; let us therefore eat and drink.
Marian, I say! a stoup of wine!

[Enter Clown]

a woman—curse the day I disguised myself! What useless sighs poor Olivia will make! Oh, time! You must untangle this, not me. It is too hard of a knot for me to untie!   [She exits.]

SCENE 3
Olivia's house.

[Enter Sir Toby and Sir Andrew.]

SIR TOBY: Come here, Sir Andrew. To be up after midnight is to be up early, and to get up at dawn is you know—

SIR ANDREW: No, I swear. I do not know. However, I know to be up late is to be up late.

SIR TOBY: That is a mistaken conclusion. I hate it like an empty wine glass. When you are up after midnight and go to bed then, it is early, so to go to bed after midnight is to go to bed early. Isn't our life made up of the four elements?

SIR ANDREW: Yes, so they say. But, on the contrary, I think it is made up of eating and drinking.

SIR TOBY: You are a scholar. Let us therefore eat and drink. Maria, I say! A cup of wine!

[Enter Feste, a Clown.]

SIR ANDREW: Here comes the fool, i' faith.

CLOWN: How now, my hearts! did you never see the picture of '
15   we three'?

SIR TOBY: Welcome, ass. Now let's have a catch.

SIR ANDREW: By my troth, the fool has an excellent breast. I had
rather than forty shillings I had such a leg, and so sweet a
breath to sing, as the fool has. In sooth, thou wast in very
20   gracious fooling last night, when thou spokest of
Pigrogromitus, of the Vapians passing the equinoctial of
Queubus: 'twas very good, i' faith. I sent thee sixpence for
thy leman: hadst it?

CLOWN: I did impeticos thy gratillity; for Malvolio's nose is no
25   whipstock: my lady has a white hand, and the Myrmidons
are no bottle-ale houses.

SIR ANDREW: Excellent! why, this is the best fooling, when all is
done. Now, a song.

SIR TOBY: Come on; there is sixpence for you: let's have a song.

30   SIR ANDREW: There's a testril of me too: if one knight give a—

CLOWN: Would you have a love-song, or a song of good life?

SIR TOBY: A love-song, a love-song.

SIR ANDREW: Ay, ay: I care not for good life.

CLOWN: *[Sings]*
35   O mistress mine, where are you roaming?
          O, stay and hear; your true love's coming,
             That can sing both high and low:
          Trip no further, pretty sweeting;
          Journeys end in lovers meeting,
40   Every wise man's son doth know.

Sɪʀ Aɴᴅʀᴇᴡ: Here comes the fool, by my word.

Cʟᴏᴡɴ: How are you, my friends! Have you ever seen the picture of "We Three"?

Sɪʀ Toʙʏ: Welcome, fool. Now, let us sing a song.

Sɪʀ Aɴᴅʀᴇᴡ: I swear, the fool has an excellent voice. I would like to have legs and a sweet singing voice like the fool, rather than have forty shillings. In truth, you were very entertaining last night when you spoke of Pigrogromitus and of the Vapians passing the equator of the Queubus. It was very good, honestly. I sent you sixpence for your girlfriend. Did you get it?

Cʟᴏᴡɴ: I did pocket your small tip, because Malvolio's nose may smell out our sins, but he cannot punish them. My sweetheart is a respectable lady, and you cannot get inexpensive ale at the Myrmidons.

Sɪʀ Aɴᴅʀᴇᴡ: Excellent! Why, this is the best humor, when all is said and done. Now, a song.

Sɪʀ Toʙʏ: Come on, here is sixpence for you. Please sing a song.

Sɪʀ Aɴᴅʀᴇᴡ: There is sixpence from me, too. If one knight gives a—

Cʟᴏᴡɴ: Do you want a love song or a song about how good life is?

Sɪʀ Toʙʏ: A love song, a love song.

Sɪʀ Aɴᴅʀᴇᴡ: Yes, yes. I do not care for good life.

Cʟᴏᴡɴ: [Sings.]
    O mistress mine, where are you roaming?
    O, stay and hear; your true love is coming,
        That can sing both high and low:
    Trip no farther, pretty sweeting;
    Journeys end in lovers meeting,
        Every wise man's son doth know.

Sir Andrew: Excellent good, i' faith.

Sir Toby: Good, good.

Clown: [Sings]
>   What is love? 'tis not hereafter;
45 >   Present mirth hath present laughter;
>   What's to come is still unsure:
>   In delay there lies no plenty;
>   Then come kiss me, sweet and twenty,
>   Youth's a stuff will not endure.

50   Sir Andrew: A mellifluous voice, as I am true knight.

Sir Toby: A contagious breath.

Sir Andrew: Very sweet and contagious, i' faith.

Sir Toby: To hear by the nose, it is dulcet in contagion. But shall
we make the welkin dance indeed? shall we rouse the
55   night-owl in a catch that will draw three souls out of one
weaver? shall we do that?

Sir Andrew: An you love me, let's do't: I am dog at a catch.

Clown: By'r lady, sir, and some dogs will catch well.

Sir Andrew: Most certain. Let our catch be, 'Thou knave.'

60   Clown: 'Hold thy peace, thou knave,' knight? I shall be
constrained in 't to call thee knave, knight.

Sir Andrew: 'Tis not the first time I have constrained one to call
me knave. Begin, fool: it begins 'Hold thy peace.'

Clown: I shall never begin if I hold my peace.

65   Sir Andrew: Good, i' faith. Come, begin. [Catch sung]

SIR ANDREW: Excellent, honestly.

SIR TOBY: Good, good.

CLOWN: [Sings.]

> What is love? 'tis not hereafter;
> Present mirth hath present laughter;
> > What's to come is still unsure:
> In delay there lies no plenty;
> Then come kiss me, sweet and twenty,
> > Youth's a stuff will not endure.

SIR ANDREW: He has a smooth voice, if I am a true knight.

SIR TOBY: It is a very infectious song.

SIR ANDREW: Very sweet and catchy, really.

SIR TOBY: When you hear by your nose, it is the sweetest infectiousness. However, should we really make the sky dance? Should we wake up the night-owl with a song that will pull three souls out of one weaver? Should we do that?

SIR ANDREW: If you love me, let's do it. I am like a dog ready to play catch.

CLOWN: By God, sir, and some dogs are good at catching.

SIR ANDREW: Most certainly. Let's have our catch be "Thou knave."

CLOWN: "Hold thy peace, thou knave," knight? I will have to call you a knave in it, knight.

SIR ANDREW: It is not the first time I have forced someone to call me a knave. You start it, fool. It begins, "Hold thy peace."

CLOWN: I will never begin if I hold my peace.

SIR ANDREW: That is good, honestly. Come on, begin. [They sing a catch.]

[Enter Maria]

MARIA: What a caterwauling do you keep here! If my lady have
not called up her steward Malvolio and bid him turn you out
of doors, never trust me.

70 SIR TOBY: My lady's a Cataian, we are politicians, Malvolio's a
Peg-a-Ramsey, and 'Three merry men be we.' Am not I
consanguineous? am I not of her blood? Tillyvally. Lady!
[Sings] 'There dwelt a man in Babylon, lady, lady!'

CLOWN: Beshrew me, the knight's in admirable fooling.

75 SIR ANDREW: Ay, he does well enough if he be disposed, and so
do I too: he does it with a better grace, but I do it more
natural.

SIR TOBY: *[Sings]* 'O, the twelfth day of December,'—

MARIA: For the love o' God, peace!

[Enter Malvolio]

80 MALVOLIO: My masters, are you mad? or what are you? Have ye
no wit, manners, nor honesty, but to gabble like tinkers at
this time of night? Do ye make an alehouse of my lady's
house, that ye squeak out your coziers' catches without any
mitigation or remorse of voice? Is there no respect of place,
persons, nor time in you?

85 SIR TOBY: We did keep time, sir, in our catches. Sneck up!

MALVOLIO: Sir Toby, I must be round with you. My lady bade me
tell you, that, though she harbours you as her kinsman, she's
nothing allied to your disorders. If you can separate yourself
and your misdemeanors, you are welcome to the house; if
90 not, an it would please you to take leave of her, she is very
willing to bid you farewell.

[Enter Maria.]

MARIA: *What a racket you are making here! I will bet anything my lady has ordered her steward, Malvolio, to kick you all out.*

SIR TOBY: *My lady is Chinese, we are clever, Malvolio is a puritan, and "Three merry men be we." Am I not related to her? Am I not of the same blood? Nonsense. Lady!* [Sings.] *"There dwelt a man in Babylon, lady, lady!"*

CLOWN: *My goodness, the knight is at his best.*

SIR ANDREW: *Yes, he is very good when he feels like it and so am I. He does it with better style, but I do it more naturally.*

SIR TOBY: [Sings.] *"O, the twelfth day of December,"*—

MARIA: *For the love of God, be quiet!*

[Enter Malvolio.]

MALVOLIO: *Gentlemen, are you out of your minds or what? Don't you have any good sense, manners, or honesty, to be babbling like beggars at this time of night? Are you trying to make a bar out of my lady's house by yelling out your nonsense songs without any restraint or shame in your voices? Don't you have any respect for where you are, other people, or what time it is?*

SIR TOBY: *We did keep time in our catches. Shut up!*

MALVOLIO: *Sir Toby, I must be blunt with you. My lady ordered me to tell you that, although she gives you a place to live because you are her uncle, she is not related to your poor behaviors. If you can end your misconduct, you are welcome to stay here. If you cannot and you would like to leave here, she is ready to bid you farewell.*

67

SIR TOBY: 'Farewell, dear heart, since I must needs be gone.'

MARIA: Nay, good Sir Toby.

CLOWN: 'His eyes do show his days are almost done.'

95 MALVOLIO: Is't even so?

SIR TOBY: 'But I will never die.'

CLOWN: Sir Toby, there you lie.

MALVOLIO: This is much credit to you.

SIR TOBY: 'Shall I bid him go?'

100 CLOWN: 'What an if you do?'

SIR TOBY: 'Shall I bid him go, and spare not?'

CLOWN: 'O no, no, no, no, you dare not.'

SIR TOBY: Out o' tune, sir: ye lie. Art any more than a steward?
Dost thou think, because thou art virtuous, there shall be no
105 more cakes and ale?

CLOWN: Yes, by Saint Anne, and ginger shall be hot i' the mouth
too.

SIR TOBY: Thou 'rt i' the right. Go, sir, rub your chain with
crumbs. A stoup of wine, Maria!

110 MALVOLIO: Mistress Mary, if you prized my lady's favour at any
thing more than contempt, you would not give means for
this uncivil rule: she shall know of it, by this hand. *[Exit]*

MARIA: Go shake your ears.

SIR TOBY: "Farewell, dear heart, since I must needs be gone."

MARIA: Stop it, good Sir Toby.

CLOWN: "His eyes do show his days are almost done."

MALVOLIO: Is that it?

SIR TOBY: "But I will never die."

CLOWN: Sir Toby, there you lie.

MALVOLIO: This is very believable.

SIR TOBY: "Shall I bid him go?"

CLOWN: "What and if you do?"

SIR TOBY: "Shall I bid him go, and spare not?"

CLOWN: "O no, no, no, no, you dare not."

SIR TOBY: You are out of tune, sir. You lie. Are you any more than a steward? Do you think, because you are pious, there will be no more parties and fun?

CLOWN: Yes, by St. Anne! And ginger will still taste hot, too.

SIR TOBY: You are right. Go and polish your chain, sir. A cup of wine, Maria!

MALVOLIO: Mistress Mary, if you care about my lady's opinion of you, you will not supply any more liquor for this disruptive behavior. She will hear about this, I swear!   [Exit.]

MARIA: Go shake your ears.

SIR ANDREW: 'Twere as good a deed as to drink when a man's a-
115   hungry, to challenge him the field, and then to break promise
with him and make a fool of him.

SIR TOBY: Do't, knight: I'll write thee a challenge: or I'll deliver
thy indignation to him by word of mouth.

MARIA: Sweet Sir Toby, be patient for tonight: since the youth of
120   the count's was today with thy lady, she is much out of quiet.
For Monsieur Malvolio, let me alone with him: if I do not
gull him into a nayword, and make him a common
recreation, do not think I have wit enough to lie straight in
my bed: I know I can do it.

125 SIR TOBY: Possess us, possess us; tell us something of him.

MARIA: Marry, sir, sometimes he is a kind of puritan.

SIR ANDREW: O, if I thought that I'ld beat him like a dog!

SIR TOBY: What, for being a puritan? thy exquisite reason, dear
knight?

130 SIR ANDREW: I have no exquisite reason for't, but I have reason
good enough.

MARIA: The devil a puritan that he is, or any thing constantly,
but a time-pleaser; an affectioned ass, that cons state without
book and utters it by great swarths: the best persuaded of
135   himself, so crammed, as he thinks, with excellencies, that it
is his grounds of faith that all that look on him love him; and
on that vice in him will my revenge find notable cause to
work.

SIR TOBY: What wilt thou do?

140 MARIA: I will drop in his way some obscure epistles of love;
wherein, by the colour of his beard, the shape of his leg, the

SIR ANDREW: *That was as good as giving a man a drink when he is hungry, and as challenging him to a duel and not showing up in order to make a fool of him.*

SIR TOBY: *Do it, knight. I will write a challenge for you, or I will deliver your insult to him by word of mouth.*

MARIA: *Sweet Sir Toby, be patient tonight. Since that count's messenger visited my lady today, she is irritable. As for Monsieur Malvolio, let me take care of him. If I do not trick him into becoming a synonym for laughing-stock and make him a fool for everyone to enjoy, do not assume I have enough brains to lie straight in my bed. I know I can do it.*

SIR TOBY: *Tell us, tell us. Tell us something about him.*

MARIA: *Well then, sir, he is sometimes kind of a puritan.*

SIR ANDREW: *Oh, if I believed that, I would beat him like a dog!*

SIR TOBY: *Why, for being a puritan? What is you excellent reason, dear knight?*

SIR ANDREW: *I have no excellent reason to do it, but I have a reason that is good enough.*

MARIA: *He is not puritan or anything else all the time. He is a follower of the current trends. He is a pretentious fool, who learns the gossip of state affairs and then recites it by the yard. He thinks that he is so full of excellent qualities that anyone who looks at him loves him. That is the weakness of his I will use to get my revenge.*

SIR TOBY: *What are you going to do?*

MARIA: *I will drop some vague love letters in his path. He will believe the letters describe him because they will contain descriptions of the color*

145 manner of his gait, the expressure of his eye, forehead, and complexion, he shall find himself most feelingly personated. I can write very like my lady your niece: on a forgotten matter we can hardly make distinction of our hands.

SIR TOBY: Excellent! I smell a device.

SIR ANDREW: I have't in my nose too.

SIR TOBY: He shall think, by the letters that thou wilt drop, that they come from my niece, and that she's in love with him.

150 MARIA: My purpose is, indeed, a horse of that colour.

SIR ANDREW: And your horse now would make him an ass.

MARIA: Ass, I doubt not.

SIR ANDREW: O, 'twill be admirable!

155 MARIA: Sport royal, I warrant you: I know my physic will work with him. I will plant you two, and let the fool make a third, where he shall find the letter: observe his construction of it. For this night, to bed, and dream on the event. Farewell.
                                                                    [Exit]

SIR TOBY: Good night, Penthesilea.

SIR ANDREW: Before me, she's a good wench.

160 SIR TOBY: She's a beagle, true-bred, and one that adores me: what o' that?

SIR ANDREW: I was adored once too.

SIR TOBY: Let's to bed, knight. Thou hadst need send for more money.

ACT II SCENE 3

of his beard, the shape of his leg, the way he walks, the look of his eyes, forehead, and complexion. I can write very similarly to my lady, your niece. With a forgotten note, sometimes we cannot tell which one of us wrote it.

SIR TOBY: Excellent! I smell a rat.

SIR ANDREW: I can smell it, too.

SIR TOBY: He will think, because of the letters you will drop, that they are from my niece and that she is in love with him.

MARIA: My purpose is similar to that, a horse of the same color.

SIR TOBY: And your horse will make him a fool.

MARIA: A fool, no doubt.

SIR ANDREW: Oh, it will be splendid!

MARIA: Royal sport, I promise you. I know my remedy will work on him. I will hide you two, and the fool, where he will find the letter. Watch his interpretation of it. For tonight, go to bed and dream about the upcoming trick. Goodnight.   [She exits.]

SIR TOBY: Goodnight, Queen of the Amazons.

SIR ANDREW: Really, she is a good woman.

SIR TOBY: She is a beagle who is thoroughbred, and she adores me. What do you think of that?

SIR ANDREW: I was adored once, too.

SIR TOBY: Let us go to bed, knight. You need to send for more money.

165   SIR ANDREW: If I cannot recover your niece, I am a foul way out.

SIR TOBY: Send for money, knight: if thou hast her not i' the end, call me cut.

SIR ANDREW: If I do not, never trust me, take it how you will.

SIR TOBY: Come, come, I'll go burn some sack; 'tis too late to go to bed now: come, knight; come, knight.

[Exeunt]

SCENE 4
Duke Orsino's palace.

[Enter Duke Orsino, Viola, Curio, and others]

DUKE ORSINO: Give me some music. Now, good morrow, friends.
Now, good Cesario, but that piece of song,
That old and antique song we heard last night:
Methought it did relieve my passion much,
5   More than light airs and recollected terms
Of these most brisk and giddy-paced times:
Come, but one verse.

CURIO: He is not here, so please your lordship that should sing it.

10   DUKE ORSINO: Who was it?

CURIO: Feste, the jester, my lord; a fool that the lady Olivia's father took much delight in. He is about the house.

DUKE ORSINO: Seek him out, and play the tune the while.
[Exit Curio. Music plays]
Come hither, boy: if ever thou shalt love,
15   In the sweet pangs of it remember me;

SIR ANDREW: *If I cannot win your niece, I am in a bind.*

SIR TOBY: *Send for the money, knight. If you do not get her in the end, call me a bobtailed horse.*

SIR ANDREW: *If I do not, never trust me. You can take that how you want.*

SIR TOBY: *Come on, come on. I will go warm up something to drink. It is too late to go to bed now. Come on, knight, come on, knight.*
[They exit.]

SCENE 4
The Duke's palace.

[Enter Duke, Viola, Curio, and others.]

DUKE: *Play me some music. Good morning, my friends. Now, good Cesario, just that bit of song, that old and delightful song, we heard last night. I thought it relieved my feelings so much more than the lighthearted and cliché songs of our fast-paced times. Please, just sing one verse.*

CURIO: *The man who sang it, so please you lord, is not here.*

DUKE: *Who was it?*

CURIO: *Feste, the jester, my lord. A fool that lady Olivia's father enjoyed greatly. He is in the house.*

DUKE: *Go find him, and in the meantime play the tune.*
[Exit Curio. Music plays.]
Come here, boy. If you should ever fall in love, remember me in the sweet torment of it. Because the way I am is the way all true lovers are,

For such as I am all true lovers are,
Unstaid and skittish in all motions else,
Save in the constant image of the creature
That is beloved. How dost thou like this tune?

20   Viola: It gives a very echo to the seat
     Where Love is throned.

Duke Orsino: Thou dost speak masterly:
     My life upon 't, young though thou art, thine eye
     Hath stay'd upon some favour that it loves:
25   Hath it not, boy?

Viola: A little, by your favour.

Duke Orsino: What kind of woman is 't?

Viola: Of your complexion.

Duke Orsino: She is not worth thee, then. What years, i' faith?

30   Viola: About your years, my lord.

Duke Orsino: Too old by heaven: let still the woman take
     An elder than herself: so wears she to him,
     So sways she level in her husband's heart:
     For, boy, however we do praise ourselves,
35   Our fancies are more giddy and unfirm,
     More longing, wavering, sooner lost and worn,
     Than women's are.

Viola: I think it well, my lord.

Duke Orsino: Then let thy love be younger than thyself,
40   Or thy affection cannot hold the bent;
     For women are as roses, whose fair flower
     Being once display'd, doth fall that very hour.

unsteady and fickle in everything, except for the constant thoughts about the ones they love. How do you like this tune?

VIOLA: It echoes the essence of love.

DUKE: You speak skillfully. I will bet my life, although you are young, that you have your eye on someone whom you love. Is it true, boy?

VIOLA: A little, if I may speak of it to you.

DUKE: What kind of woman is it?

VIOLA: She looks like you.

DUKE: She is not worthy of you then. How old is she?

VIOLA: About your age, my lord.

DUKE: By heaven, she is too old for you. A woman should marry a man who is older than she is, so that she adapts to suit him, and, therefore, her husband's love remains constant to her. Because, boy, no matter how men praise themselves, our love is more fickle and unsteady, more desirous and inconstant, and sooner worn out and lost than women's love is.

VIOLA: I believe it, my lord.

DUKE: So love someone younger than yourself, or your love will not last, because women are like roses. Once their beautiful flower blooms, it falls that same hour.

VIOLA: And so they are: alas, that they are so;
    To die, even when they to perfection grow!

[Re-enter Curio and Clown]

45   DUKE ORSINO: O, fellow, come, the song we had last night.
    Mark it, Cesario, it is old and plain;
    The spinsters and the knitters in the sun
    And the free maids that weave their thread with bones
    Do use to chant it: it is silly sooth,
50   And dallies with the innocence of love,
    Like the old age.

CLOWN: Are you ready, sir?

DUKE ORSINO: Ay; prithee, sing.   *[Music]*

SONG.

CLOWN: Come away, come away, death,
55   And in sad cypress let me be laid;
    Fly away, fly away breath;
    I am slain by a fair cruel maid.
    My shroud of white, stuck all with yew,
    O, prepare it!
60   My part of death, no one so true
    Did share it.

    Not a flower, not a flower sweet
    On my black coffin let there be strown;
    Not a friend, not a friend greet
65   My poor corpse, where my bones shall be thrown:
    A thousand thousand sighs to save,
    Lay me, O, where
    Sad true lover never find my grave,
    To weep there!

70   DUKE ORSINO: There's for thy pains.

CLOWN: No pains, sir: I take pleasure in singing, sir.

VIOLA: *Yes, they are. It is sad that they are like that. They die just as they reach perfection!*

[Re-enter Curio and Feste, a Clown.]

DUKE: *Oh, fellow, come here and sing that song we heard last night. Listen to it, Cesario. It is old and plain. Spinners and knitters in the sunshine and the single maids that make lace frequently sing it. It is simple truthfulness, and it discusses the innocence of love in past times.*

CLOWN: *Are you ready, sir?*

DUKE: *Yes, please sing.* [Music.]

CLOWN: SONG
Come away, come away, death,
  And in sad cypress let me be laid;
Fly away, fly away, breath;
  I am slain by a fair cruel maid.
My shroud of white, stuck all with yew,
    O, prepare it!
My part of death, no one so true
    Did share it.

Not a flower, not a flower sweet,
  On my black coffin let there be strown;
Not a friend, not a friend greet
  My poor corpse, where my bones shall be thrown:
A thousand thousand sighs to save,
    Lay me, O, where
Sad true lover never find my grave,
    To weep there!

DUKE: *Here is money for your trouble.*

CLOWN: *It is no trouble, sir. I enjoy singing it, sir.*

DUKE ORSINO: I'll pay thy pleasure then.

CLOWN: Truly, sir, and pleasure will be paid, one time or another.

DUKE ORSINO: Give me now leave to leave thee.

75 CLOWN: Now, the melancholy god protect thee; and the tailor
make thy doublet of changeable taffeta, for thy mind is a very
opal. I would have men of such constancy put to sea, that
their business might be every thing and their intent every
where; for that's it that always makes a good voyage of
80 nothing. Farewell. *[Exit]*

DUKE ORSINO: Let all the rest give place.
[Curio and Attendants retire]
Once more, Cesario,
Get thee to yond same sovereign cruelty:
Tell her, my love, more noble than the world,
85 Prizes not quantity of dirty lands;
The parts that fortune hath bestow'd upon her,
Tell her, I hold as giddily as fortune;
But 'tis that miracle and queen of gems
That nature pranks her in attracts my soul.

90 VIOLA: But if she cannot love you, sir?

DUKE ORSINO: I cannot be so answer'd.

VIOLA: Sooth, but you must.
Say that some lady, as perhaps there is,
Hath for your love a great a pang of heart
95 As you have for Olivia: you cannot love her;
You tell her so; must she not then be answer'd?

DUKE ORSINO: There is no woman's sides
Can bide the beating of so strong a passion
As love doth give my heart; no woman's heart
100 So big, to hold so much; they lack retention

DUKE: *I will pay you for your pleasure then.*

CLOWN: *Yes, sir. The pleasure must be paid sometimes.*

DUKE: *Please allow me to ask you to leave now.*

CLOWN: *May the god of melancholy protect you, and your tailor make your jacket of different shades of taffeta, because your mind is like an opal. I would put men with that inconstancy to sea, so that their business would be everything, and their aim, everywhere. That is how a good voyage is made, by having no destination. Goodbye.* [He exits.]

DUKE: *Everyone else may go.*
                         [Curio and attendants leave.]
Once more, Cesario, go to that supreme cruelty. Tell her my love, which is nobler than the world, does not want large amounts of squalid land. Tell her what good fortune has given her, I see as inconsequential luck. What attracts me to her is her beauty, which is a miracle and makes her a queen of gems.

VIOLA: *What if she cannot love you, sir?*

DUKE: *I cannot accept that answer.*

VIOLA: *Really, you must. Imagine there is some lady, as maybe there is, who loves you as painfully as you love Olivia. You cannot love her. You tell her that. Doesn't she have to accept that answer?*

DUKE: *There is no woman's body that could handle the beating of such a strong passion that love has put in my heart. No woman's heart is big enough to hold this much love. Women lack the power to keep emotion. Indeed, their love could be called appetite. It does not come from their*

Alas, their love may be call'd appetite,
No motion of the liver, but the palate,
That suffer surfeit, cloyment and revolt;
But mine is all as hungry as the sea,
105   And can digest as much: make no compare
Between that love a woman can bear me
And that I owe Olivia.

VIOLA: Ay, but I know—

DUKE ORSINO: What dost thou know?

110 VIOLA: Too well what love women to men may owe:
In faith, they are as true of heart as we.
My father had a daughter loved a man,
As it might be, perhaps, were I a woman,
I should your lordship.

115 DUKE ORSINO: And what's her history?

VIOLA: A blank, my lord. She never told her love,
But let concealment, like a worm i' the bud,
Feed on her damask cheek: she pined in thought,
And with a green and yellow melancholy
120   She sat like patience on a monument,
Smiling at grief. Was not this love indeed?
We men may say more, swear more: but indeed
Our shows are more than will; for still we prove
Much in our vows, but little in our love.

125 DUKE ORSINO: But died thy sister of her love, my boy?

VIOLA: I am all the daughters of my father's house,
And all the brothers too: and yet I know not.
Sir, shall I to this lady?

DUKE ORSINO: Ay, that's the theme.
130   To her in haste; give her this jewel; say,
My love can give no place, bide no denay.   *[Exeunt]*

passions, but their taste. They can have too much, gorge themselves, and then feel revulsion. My appetite is as hungry as the sea, and it can digest as much. Do not make a comparison between the love a woman can have for me and the love that I have for Olivia.

VIOLA: *Yes, but I know—*

DUKE: *What do you know?*

VIOLA: *Too well how much women can love men. In truth, they are as faithful as we are. My father had a daughter who loved a man, just as perhaps, if I were a woman, I would love your lordship.*

DUKE: *And what is her story?*

VIOLA: *A blank, my lord. She never told her love, but let the secret, like a worm in a bud, destroy the color in her cheeks. She obsessed over him in her thoughts, and made herself sick with longing. She sat like a statue of patience on a monument, smiling at her grief. Wasn't this truly love? We men may say more, swear more, but really, our actions are a show. We tend to take many vows, but love too little.*

DUKE: *Did your sister die of her love, my boy?*

VIOLA: *I am the daughters of my father's house, and all the brothers too, but I do not know. Sir, should I go to this lady?*

DUKE: *Yes, that is what we were talking about. Go to her quickly, and give her this jewel. Tell her my love cannot accept or endure a refusal.*
                                        [They exit.]

SCENE 5
Olivia's garden.

[Enter Sir Toby, Sir Andrew, and Fabian]

Sir Toby: Come thy ways, Signior Fabian.

Fabian: Nay, I'll come: if I lose a scruple of this sport, let me be boiled to death with melancholy.

5 Sir Toby: Wouldst thou not be glad to have the niggardly rascally sheep-biter come by some notable shame?

Fabian: I would exult, man: you know, he brought me out o' favour with my lady about a bear-baiting here.

Sir Toby: To anger him we'll have the bear again; and we will fool him black and blue: shall we not, Sir Andrew?

10 Sir Andrew: An we do not, it is pity of our lives.

Sir Toby: Here comes the little villain.

[Enter Maria]
How now, my metal of India!

Maria: Get ye all three into the box-tree: Malvolio's coming down this walk: he has been yonder i' the sun practising
15 behavior to his own shadow this half hour: observe him, for the love of mockery; for I know this letter will make a con templative idiot of him. Close, in the name of jesting! Lie thou there, *[Throws down a letter]* for here comes the trout that must be caught with tickling. *[Exit]*

[Enter Malvolio]

20 Malvolio: 'Tis but fortune; all is fortune. Maria once told me she did affect me: and I have heard herself come thus near, that,

SCENE 5
Olivia's garden.

[Enter Sir Toby, Sir Andrew, and Fabian.]

SIR TOBY: *Come this way, Mr. Fabian.*

FABIAN: *Oh, I am coming. If I miss a minute of this trick, I will die of depression.*

SIR TOBY: *Wouldn't you be glad to have that stingy, rascally, vicious dog put to shame?*

FABIAN: *I would celebrate, man. You know he got me in trouble with my lady over a bear-baiting that was held here.*

SIR TOBY: *To make him mad we will have the bear-baiting here again, and we will fool him excellently. Won't we, Sir Andrew?*

SIR ANDREW: *If we do not, we will regret it for the rest of our lives.*

SIR TOBY: *Here comes the little villain.*

[Enter Maria.]
   How are you, my treasure?

MARIA: *All of you get behind those thick bushes. Malvolio's coming down this path. He has been outside practicing behavior by himself for the last half hour. Watch him, for your love of making fun of him, because I know this letter will make him a complete idiot. Keep down, in the name of joking.* [She throws down a letter.] *Here comes the trout that will be caught by flattery.*   [She exits.]

[Enter Malvolio.]

MALVOLIO: *It is only luck. Everything is luck. Maria once told me Olivia cared for me, and I have heard her say something very similar. She said* should she fancy, it should be one of my complexion. Besides, she uses me with a more exalted respect than any one else that follows her. What should I think on 't?

25 SIR TOBY: Here's an overweening rogue!

FABIAN: O, peace! Contemplation makes a rare turkey-cock of him: how he jets under his advanced plumes!

SIR ANDREW: 'Slight, I could so beat the rogue!

SIR TOBY: Peace, I say.

30 MALVOLIO: To be Count Malvolio!

SIR TOBY: Ah, rogue!

SIR ANDREW: Pistol him, pistol him.

SIR TOBY: Peace, peace!

MALVOLIO: There is example for't; the lady of the Strachy
35   married the yeoman of the wardrobe.

SIR ANDREW: Fie on him, Jezebel!

FABIAN: O, peace! now he's deeply in: look how imagination blows him.

MALVOLIO: Having been three months married to her, sitting in
40   my state,—

SIR TOBY: O, for a stone-bow, to hit him in the eye!

MALVOLIO: Calling my officers about me, in my branched velvet gown; having come from a day-bed, where I have left Olivia sleeping,—

if she fell in love with someone, he would be like me. Besides, she treats me with more respect than anyone else that seeks her love. What should I think?

SIR TOBY: Here is an arrogant lowlife!

FABIAN: Oh, be quiet! Thinking turns him into a rare peacock. Look how he struts under his uplifted feathers!

SIR ANDREW: I swear, I could really beat up the lowlife!

SIR TOBY: Be quiet, I say.

MALVOLIO: I could be Count Malvolio!

SIR TOBY: Oh, vagrant!

SIR ANDREW: Shoot him, shoot him.

SIR TOBY: Quiet, quiet!

MALVOLIO: It has happened before. The lady of Strachy married her wardrobe man.

SIR ANDREW: Curse him, Jezebel!

FABIAN: Oh, be quiet! Now he is really daydreaming. Look how his imaginings make him swell with pride.

MALVOLIO: After being married to her for three months, sitting on my throne—

SIR TOBY: Oh, if only I had a crossbow so that I could shoot him in the eye!

MALVOLIO: I would be calling my servants to me, while wearing my velvet, elaborate gown, after leaving Olivia sleeping on our sofa—

45   SIR TOBY: Fire and brimstone!

FABIAN: O, peace, peace!

MALVOLIO: And then to have the humour of state; and after a
    demure travel of regard, telling them I know my place as I
    would they should do theirs, to for my kinsman Toby,—

50   SIR TOBY: Bolts and shackles!

FABIAN: O peace, peace, peace! now, now.

MALVOLIO: Seven of my people, with an obedient start, make out
    for him: I frown the while; and perchance wind up watch, or
    play with my—some rich jewel. Toby approaches; courtesies
55   there to me,—

SIR TOBY: Shall this fellow live?

FABIAN: Though our silence be drawn from us with cars, yet
    peace.

MALVOLIO: I extend my hand to him thus, quenching my familiar
60   smile with an austere regard of control,—

SIR TOBY: And does not Toby take you a blow o' the lips then?

MALVOLIO: Saying, 'Cousin Toby, my fortunes having cast me on
    your niece give me this prerogative of speech,'—

SIR TOBY: What, what?

65   MALVOLIO: 'You must amend your drunkenness.'

SIR TOBY: Out, scab!

FABIAN: Nay, patience, or we break the sinews of our plot.

SIR TOBY: *May you suffer in hell!*

FABIAN: *Oh, quiet, quiet!*

MALVOLIO: *Then I would be in the mood for state affairs, and after solemnly examining them all, I would tell them, I know my place and hope that they know theirs. Then I would ask for my kinsman Toby—*

SIR TOBY: *Arrest him!*

FABIAN: *Oh, quiet, quiet, quiet! Calm down, now.*

MALVOLIO: *Seven of my servants, attending to me obediently, go to look for him. I frown while I wait, and maybe wind up my watch or play with my—some rich jewel. Toby comes and bows to me—*

SIR TOBY: *Should I let this man live?*

FABIAN: *Even if a team of horses tried to drag words out of us, we must be quiet.*

MALVOLIO: *I extend my hand to him like this, replacing my usual smile with a stern look of authority—*

SIR TOBY: *And doesn't Toby then punch you in the mouth?*

MALVOLIO: *Saying, "Cousin Toby, my luck having given me your niece, I now have the right to say—"*

SIR TOBY: *What, what?*

MALVOLIO: *"You must stop your excessive drinking."*

SIR TOBY: *Get out, you scab!*

FABIAN: *No, have patience, or we will ruin our plot.*

MALVOLIO: 'Besides, you waste the treasure of your time with a foolish knight,'—

70 SIR ANDREW: That's me, I warrant you.

MALVOLIO: 'One Sir Andrew,'—

SIR ANDREW: I knew 'twas I; for many do call me fool.

MALVOLIO: What employment have we here?
[Taking up the letter]

FABIAN: Now is the woodcock near the gin.

75 SIR TOBY: O, peace! and the spirit of humour intimate reading aloud to him!

MALVOLIO: By my life, this is my lady's hand these be her very C's, her U's and her T's and thus makes she her great P's. It is, in contempt of question, her hand.

80 SIR ANDREW: Her C's, her U's and her T's: why that?

MALVOLIO: [Reads] 'To the unknown beloved, this, and my good wishes:'—her very phrases! By your leave, wax. Soft! and the impressure her Lucrece, with which she uses to seal: 'tis my lady. To whom should this be?

85 FABIAN: This wins him, liver and all.

MALVOLIO: [Reads]   Jove knows I love:
                        But who?
                  Lips, do not move;
                  No man must know.
90 'No man must know.' What follows? the numbers altered! 'No man must know:' if this should be thee, Malvolio?

MALVOLIO: "Besides, you waste your valuable time with a foolish knight—"

SIR ANDREW: He is talking about me, I guarantee you.

MALVOLIO: "One Sir Andrew—"

SIR ANDREW: I knew he was talking about me, because many people do call me a fool.

MALVOLIO: What business do we have here? [Picking up the letter.]

FABIAN: Now the bird is near our trap.

SIR TOBY: Oh, be quiet! Spirits of moods, urge him to read it aloud.

MALVOLIO: I would bet my life that this is my lady's handwriting. These are her C's, her U's, and her T's. And this is how she writes her capital P's. It is, undoubtedly, her handwriting.

SIR ANDREW: Her C's, her U's, and her T's, what does he mean?

MALVOLIO: [Reads.] "To the unknown beloved, this, and my good wishes." This is exactly the way she speaks! With your permission, wax. Gently! And the wax was sealed with a picture of Lucrece, which is what Olivia uses to seal letters. This was written by my lady. For whom is this letter meant?

FABIAN: This is convincing him completely.

MALVOLIO: [Reads.]   God knows I love:
                           But who?
                        Lips, do not move;
                        No man must know.
"No man must know." What comes next? The meter changes! "No man must know:" Could it by you, Malvolio?

SIR TOBY: Marry, hang thee, brock!

MALVOLIO: *[Reads]*   I may command where I adore;
                    But silence, like a Lucrece knife,
95   With bloodless stroke my heart doth gore:
                    M, O, A, I, doth sway my life.

FABIAN: A fustian riddle!

SIR TOBY: Excellent wench, say I.

MALVOLIO: 'M, O, A, I, doth sway my life.' Nay, but first, let me
100   see, let me see, let me see.

FABIAN: What dish o' poison has she dressed him!

SIR TOBY: And with what wing the staniel cheques at it!

MALVOLIO: 'I may command where I adore.' Why, she may
       command me: I serve her; she is my lady. Why, this is
105   evident to any formal capacity; there is no obstruction in
       this: and the end,—what should that alphabetical position
       portend? If I could make that resemble something in me,—
       Softly! M, O, A, I,—

SIR TOBY: O, ay, make up that: he is now at a cold scent.

110 FABIAN: Sowter will cry upon't for all this, though it be as rank as
       a fox.

MALVOLIO: M,—Malvolio; M,—why, that begins my name.

FABIAN: Did not I say he would work it out? the cur is excellent
       at faults.

115 MALVOLIO: M,—but then there is no consonancy in the sequel;
       that suffers under probation A should follow but O does.

SIR TOBY: *I hope you are hanged, you rat!*

MALVOLIO: [Reads.]   *I may command where I adore;*
                            But silence, like Lucrece's knife,
                            With a bloodless stroke deeply wounds my heart:
                            M, O, A, I, sways my life.

FABIAN: *A ridiculous riddle!*

SIR TOBY: *What an excellent woman.*

MALVOLIO: *"M, O, A, I, sways my life." Yes, but first, let me think, let me think, let me think.*

FABIAN: *What a dish of poison she has given him!*

SIR TOBY: *And look how quickly the hawk has swooped down on the bait!*

MALVOLIO: *"I may command where I adore." Well, she commands me. I serve her. She is my lady. Why, this is clear to anyone with a decent mind. There is no difficulty in understanding this. And her purpose; what does the arrangement of letters mean? If I could make that also indicate me. Gently! "M, O, A, I.*

SIR TOBY: *Oh, yes, look at that. Now he is losing the scent.*

FABIAN: *Despite that, the incompetent dog will find the scent again, even though it has stunk like a fox since the beginning.*

MALVOLIO: *M,—Malvolio. M,—why, that is the first letter of my name.*

FABIAN: *Didn't I say he would figure it out? The dog is very good at losing and then finding scents.*

MALVOLIO: *M,—but then there is no regularity in the sequence. It falls apart under scrutiny. A should follow, but O does.*

FABIAN: And O shall end, I hope.

SIR TOBY: Ay, or I'll cudgel him, and make him cry O!

MALVOLIO: And then I comes behind.

120 FABIAN: Ay, an you had any eye behind you, you might see more detraction at your heels than fortunes before you.

MALVOLIO: M, O, A, I; this simulation is not as the former: and yet, to crush this a little, it would bow to me, for every one of these letters are in my name. Soft! here follows prose.

125 *[Reads]* 'If this fall into thy hand, revolve. In my stars I am above thee; but be not afraid of greatness: some are born great, some achieve greatness, and some have greatness thrust upon 'em. Thy Fates open their hands; let thy blood and spirit embrace them; and, to inure thyself to what thou art like to be, cast thy humble slough
130 and appear fresh. Be opposite with a kinsman, surly with servants; let thy tongue tang arguments of state; put thyself into the trick of singularity: she thus advises thee that sighs for thee. Remember who commended thy yellow stockings, and wished to see thee ever cross-gartered: I say, remember. Go to, thou art made, if thou
135 desirest to be so; if not, let me see thee a steward still, the fellow of servants, and not worthy to touch Fortune's fingers.
Farewell.
She that would alter services with thee,
THE FORTUNATE-UNHAPPY.'
140 Daylight and champaign discovers not more: this is open. I will be proud, I will read politic authors, I will baffle Sir Toby, I will wash off gross acquaintance, I will be point-devise the very man. I do not now fool myself, to let imagination jade me; for every reason excites to this, that my lady loves me.
145 She did commend my yellow stockings of late, she did praise my leg being cross-gartered; and in this she manifests herself to my love, and with a kind of injunction drives me to these habits of her liking. I thank my stars I am happy. I will be strange, stout, in yellow stockings, and cross-gartered, even
150 with the swiftness of putting on. Jove and my stars be

FABIAN: *And O will end it, I hope.*

SIR TOBY: *Yes, or I will beat him up to make him cry out, O!*

MALVOLIO: *And then I comes next.*

FABIAN: *Yes, and if you had an eye in the back of your head, you would see more trouble at your heels than good fortune in your future.*

MALVOLIO: *M, O, A, I, this riddle is not like the earlier one. Yet, if I twist this a little, it would indicate me, because every one of these letters are in my name. Oh! There is writing afterward.*

[Reads.] *"If this falls into your hand, contemplate. In my stars, I am above you; but do not be afraid of greatness: some are born great, some achieve greatness, and some have greatness thrust upon them. The Fates offer their hands; let your passion and spirit embrace them; and accustom yourself to what you are likely to be. Shed your humble outer skin and appear fresh. Be quarrelsome with a kinsman, surly with servants; let your tongue discuss important matters; put yourself into the practice of individualism: she who gives you this advice also sighs for you. Remember who complimented your yellow stockings, and wished to see you always cross-gartered: I say, remember. Go ahead, you are made, if you desire to be so; if not, let me see you act like a steward always, the fellow of servants, and not worthy to touch Fortune's fingers. Farewell. She that would be your servant,*

THE FORTUNATE-UNHAPPY."

It is as clear as daylight and the open county. This is very straightforward. I will be proud. I will read clever authors. I will argue with Sir Toby. I will reject my lower ranking friends. I will do exactly as the letter says. I will be that man. I am not deceiving myself and letting my imagination humiliate me. Everything indicates that my lady loves me. She did compliment my yellow stockings recently, and she did say she liked it when my legs were cross-gartered. In this letter, she definitely shows that she loves me, and heavily encourages me to do the things that she likes. I thank my lucky stars that I am so fortunate. I will be aloof and arrogant. I will wear yellow stockings and cross-garters, as fast as I can get them on. Praise God and my luck! There is also a post script.

praised! Here is yet a postscript.

[Reads] 'Thou canst not choose but know who I am. If thou entertainest my love, let it appear in thy smiling; thy smiles become thee well; therefore in my presence still smile, dear my sweet, I

155   prithee.'

Jove, I thank thee: I will smile; I will do everything that thou wilt have me.   *[Exit]*

FABIAN: I will not give my part of this sport for a pension of thousands to be paid from the Sophy.

160 SIR TOBY: I could marry this wench for this device.

SIR ANDREW: So could I too.

SIR TOBY: And ask no other dowry with her but such another jest.

SIR ANDREW: Nor I neither.

165 FABIAN: Here comes my noble gull-catcher.

[Re-enter Maria]

SIR TOBY: Wilt thou set thy foot o' my neck?

SIR ANDREW: Or o' mine either?

SIR TOBY: Shall I play my freedom at traytrip, and become thy bond-slave?

170 SIR ANDREW: I' faith, or I either?

SIR TOBY: Why, thou hast put him in such a dream, that when the image of it leaves him he must run mad.

MARIA: Nay, but say true; does it work upon him?

[Reads.] *You cannot help but know who I am. If you accept my love, let it appear in your smiling; your smiles are attractive; therefore, in my presence always smile, dear my sweet, I beg you."*

God, I thank you. I will smile. I will do everything that you want me to do. [Exit.]

FABIAN: *I would not give up getting to see this trick for a pension worth thousands, to be paid by the Shah of Persia.*

SIR TOBY: *I could marry this woman for creating this trick.*

SIR ANDREW: *So could I.*

SIR TOBY: *And I would not ask for a dowry from her, except that she come up with another trick.*

SIR ANDREW: *Me neither.*

FABIAN: *Here comes our noble prankster.*

[Re-enter Maria.]

SIR TOBY: *Will you put your foot on my neck?*

SIR ANDREW: *Or on mine?*

SIR TOBY: *Should I bet my freedom on a dice game with you and become your slave?*

SIR ANDREW: *Yes, or should I?*

SIR TOBY: *Well, you have put him into such a fantasy that when he discovers it is not true he will go crazy.*

MARIA: *Oh, tell me if it is true. Did it work on him?*

SIR TOBY: Like aqua-vitae with a midwife.

175 MARIA: If you will then see the fruits of the sport, mark his first approach before my lady: he will come to her in yellow stockings, and 'tis a colour she abhors, and cross-gartered, a fashion she detests; and he will smile upon her, which will now be so unsuitable to her disposition, being addicted to a
180 melancholy as she is, that it cannot but turn him into a notable contempt. If you will see it, follow me.

SIR TOBY: To the gates of Tartar, thou most excellent devil of wit!

SIR ANDREW: I'll make one too.

[Exeunt]

SIR TOBY: *Like strong liquor on a midwife.*

MARIA: *If you want to see the results of this joke, watch his first meeting with Olivia. He will come to her in yellow stockings, a color that she hates, and cross-gartered, a fashion she despises. He will smile at her, which will be so completely inappropriate, because she is sad and in mourning, that she will become very annoyed with him. If you want to see it, follow me.*

SIR TOBY: *Take us to the gates of Hell, you excellent devil of cleverness!*

SIR ANDREW: *I will come, too.*

[They exit.]

ACT III

SCENE 1
Olivia's garden.

[Enter Viola, and Clown with a tabour]

VIOLA: Save thee, friend, and thy music: dost thou live by thy tabour?

CLOWN: No, sir, I live by the church.

VIOLA: Art thou a churchman?

5   CLOWN: No such matter, sir: I do live by the church; for I do live at my house, and my house doth stand by the church.

VIOLA: So thou mayst say, the king lies by a beggar, if a beggar dwell near him; or, the church stands by thy tabour, if thy tabour stand by the church.

10   CLOWN: You have said, sir. To see this age! A sentence is but a cheveril glove to a good wit: how quickly the wrong side may be turned outward!

VIOLA: Nay, that's certain; they that dally nicely with words may quickly make them wanton.

15   CLOWN: I would, therefore, my sister had had no name, sir.

VIOLA: Why, man?

ACT III

SCENE 1
Olivia's garden.

[Enter Viola and Feste, a Clown, with a small drum.]

VIOLA: *Greetings to you, friend, and to your music. Do you live by drumming?*

CLOWN: *No, sir. I live by the church.*

VIOLA: *Are you a clergyman?*

CLOWN: *No, I am not, sir. I live by the church, because I live at my house, and my house is next to the church.*

VIOLA: *So you might say, the king lives by begging, if a beggar lives near him. Or, the church is near the drumming, if your drum is near the church.*

CLOWN: *You are right, sir. That is the way the current times are! A saying is like a flexible leather glove to a smart man. It is easy to turn inside out!*

VIOLA: *Yes, that is for sure. Those who are clever with words can quickly give them lewd meanings.*

CLOWN: *I wish my sister did not have a name because of that.*

VIOLA: *Why, man?*

CLOWN: Why, sir, her name's a word; and to dally with that word might make my sister wanton. But indeed words are very rascals since bonds disgraced them.

20   VIOLA: Thy reason, man?

CLOWN: Troth, sir, I can yield you none without words; and words are grown so false, I am loath to prove reason with them.

VIOLA: I warrant thou art a merry fellow and carest for nothing.

25   CLOWN: Not so, sir, I do care for something; but in my conscience, sir, I do not care for you: if that be to care for nothing, sir, I would it would make you invisible.

VIOLA: Art not thou the Lady Olivia's fool?

CLOWN: No, indeed, sir; the Lady Olivia has no folly: she will
30   keep no fool, sir, till she be married; and fools are as like husbands as pilchards are to herrings; the husband's the bigger: I am indeed not her fool, but her corrupter of words.

VIOLA: I saw thee late at the Count Orsino's.

CLOWN: Foolery, sir, does walk about the orb like the sun, it
35   shines every where. I would be sorry, sir, but the fool should be as oft with your master as with my mistress: I think I saw your wisdom there.

VIOLA: Nay, an thou pass upon me, I'll no more with thee. Hold, there's expenses for thee.

40   CLOWN: Now Jove, in his next commodity of hair, send thee a beard!

VIOLA: By my troth, I'll tell thee, I am almost sick for one; [Aside] though I would not have it grow on my chin. Is thy lady within?

CLOWN: Well, sir, her name is a word, and if you play with that word, it could make my sister lewd. Indeed, words have become worthless since we must use bonds to guarantee words' meanings.

VIOLA: Why do you think that, man?

CLOWN: Truly, sir, I cannot tell you without using words, and words have become so undependable I am unwilling to prove my reasons with them.

VIOLA: I bet you are a happy fellow with no worries.

CLOWN: No I am not, sir. I do care about something, but on my word, sir, I do not care about you. If that means I do not care about anything, sir, I wish it would make you invisible.

VIOLA: Aren't you Lady Olivia's fool?

CLOWN: No, I am not, sir. The Lady Olivia has no entertainment. She will not have a fool, sir, until she is married. Fools are to husbands as sardines are to herrings; the husband is bigger. No, I am not her fool, but I am her corrupter of words.

VIOLA: I saw you recently at the Count Orsino's court.

CLOWN: Foolery, sir, does go around the world like the sun. It shines every-where. I would be sorry, sir, if the fool were not with your master as often as he is with my mistress. I think I saw you there.

VIOLA: Well, if you make fun of me, I will not want to talk with you anymore. Wait, here is some money for you.

CLOWN: When God gets more beards in, let him send you one!

VIOLA: I swear, I will tell you, I am almost sick over one. [Aside.] However, I do not want it to grow on my chin. Is the lady home?

45   Clown: Would not a pair of these have bred, sir?

Viola: Yes, being kept together and put to use.

Clown: I would play Lord Pandarus of Phrygia, sir, to bring a
    Cressida to this Troilus.

Viola: I understand you, sir; 'tis well begged.

50   Clown: The matter, I hope, is not great, sir, begging but a
    beggar: Cressida was a beggar. My lady is within, sir. I will
    construe to them whence you come; who you are and what
    you would are out of my welkin, I might say 'element,' but
    the word is over-worn.   *[Exit]*

55   Viola: This fellow is wise enough to play the fool;
    And to do that well craves a kind of wit:
    He must observe their mood on whom he jests,
    The quality of persons, and the time,
    And, like the haggard, cheque at every feather
60   That comes before his eye. This is a practise
    As full of labour as a wise man's art
    For folly that he wisely shows is fit;
    But wise men, folly-fall'n, quite taint their wit.

[Enter Sir Toby, and Sir Andrew]

Sir Toby: Save you, gentleman.

65   Viola: And you, sir.

Sir Andrew: Dieu vous garde, monsieur.

Viola: Et vous aussi; votre serviteur.

Sir Andrew: I hope, sir, you are; and I am yours.

CLOWN: Wouldn't a pair of these buy me more, sir?

VIOLA: Yes, if you save them and put them to good use.

CLOWN: I would like to be Lord Pandarus of Phrygia, sir, and bring a Cressida to this Troilus.

VIOLA: I understand what you mean, sir. You have begged for it well.

CLOWN: My begging because I am a beggar is not wrong, I hope, sir. Cressida was a beggar. My lady is home, sir. I will tell them where you have come from. Who you are and what you want are out of my sky. I could use the word "element" but it is overused.   [He exits.]

VIOLA: This man is wise enough to be a jester, and to do that requires a certain intelligence. He must evaluate the mood of the people for whom he is performing, what type of people they are, and the occasion. He cannot, like a wild hawk, grab at every piece of bait that comes to him. His profession requires as much training as a wise man's. Joking that is done with wisdom is appropriate, but wise men who use fooling tarnish their reputations.

[Enter Sir Toby and Sir Andrew.]

SIR TOBY: God save you, sir.

VIOLA: And you, too, sir.

SIR ANDREW: God keep you, sir.

VIOLA: And you, too. I am your servant.

SIR ANDREW: I hope you are, sir, and I am yours.

SIR TOBY: Will you encounter the house? my niece is desirous
70   you should enter, if your trade be to her.

VIOLA: I am bound to your niece, sir; I mean, she is the list of
    my voyage.

SIR TOBY: Taste your legs, sir; put them to motion.

VIOLA: My legs do better understand me, sir, than I understand
75   what you mean by bidding me taste my legs.

SIR TOBY: I mean, to go, sir, to enter.

VIOLA: I will answer you with gait and entrance. But we are
    prevented.

[Enter Olivia and Maria]
    Most excellent accomplished lady, the heavens rain odours
80   on you!

SIR ANDREW: That youth's a rare courtier: 'Rain odours;' well.

VIOLA: My matter hath no voice, to your own most pregnant and
    vouchsafed ear.

SIR ANDREW: 'Odours,' 'pregnant' and 'vouchsafed:' I'll get 'em
85   all three all ready.

OLIVIA: Let the garden door be shut, and leave me to my hearing.
                    [Exeunt Sir Toby, Sir Andrew, and Maria]
    Give me your hand, sir.

VIOLA: My duty, madam, and most humble service.

OLIVIA: What is your name?

90 VIOLA: Cesario is your servant's name, fair princess.

SIR TOBY: *Would you like to enter the house? My niece would like you to come in, if you are here to speak with her.*

VIOLA: *I am headed toward your niece, sir. I mean, she is the purpose of my trip.*

SIR TOBY: *Try your legs, sir. Put them into motion.*

VIOLA: *My legs understand me better, sir, than I understand what you mean when you tell me to try my legs.*

SIR TOBY: *I mean, go in, sir, enter.*

VIOLA: *I will respond to you by walking and going in. However, we are stopped.*

[Enter Olivia and Maria.]
Most excellent, accomplished lady, may the heavens rain odors on you!

SIR ANDREW: *That young man is an excellent flatterer. "Rain odors," indeed.*

VIOLA: *I will only say what I have come to say in the sole presence of your pregnant and vouchsafed ear.*

SIR ANDREW: *"Odors," "pregnant," and "vouchsafed." I must remember all three of them.*

OLIVIA: *Close the garden door and leave me to listen to this.*
                          [Exit Sir Toby, Sir Andrew, and Maria.]
Give me you hand, sir.

VIOLA: *I do it as my duty and most modest service, madam.*

OLIVIA: *What is your name?*

VIOLA: *Cesario is your servant's name, beautiful princess.*

OLIVIA: My servant, sir! 'Twas never merry world
    Since lowly feigning was call'd compliment:
    You're servant to the Count Orsino, youth.

VIOLA: And he is yours, and his must needs be yours:
95   Your servant's servant is your servant, madam.

OLIVIA: For him, I think not on him: for his thoughts,
    Would they were blanks, rather than fill'd with me!

VIOLA: Madam, I come to whet your gentle thoughts
    On his behalf.

100 OLIVIA: O, by your leave, I pray you,
    I bade you never speak again of him:
    But, would you undertake another suit,
    I had rather hear you to solicit that
    Than music from the spheres.

105 VIOLA: Dear lady,—

OLIVIA: Give me leave, beseech you. I did send,
    After the last enchantment you did here,
    A ring in chase of you: so did I abuse
    Myself, my servant and, I fear me, you:
110   Under your hard construction must I sit,
    To force that on you, in a shameful cunning,
    Which you knew none of yours: what might you think?
    Have you not set mine honour at the stake
    And baited it with all the unmuzzled thoughts
115   That tyrannous heart can think? To one of your receiving
    Enough is shown: a cypress, not a bosom,
    Hideth my heart. So, let me hear you speak.

VIOLA: I pity you.

OLIVIA: That's a degree to love.

Olivia: *My servant, sir! It is a sad world when lies are given as compliments. You are Count Orsino's servant, young man.*

Viola: *And he is your servant, so what he has is yours. Your servant's servant is your servant, madam.*

Olivia: *As for him, I do not think about him. It would be better if he had no thoughts than to have them filled with me.*

Viola: *Madam, I come to encourage you to think of him more kindly.*

Olivia: *Oh, with your permission, please. I requested you never visit me about him again. However, if you are going to try to win me again, I would rather hear it come from you than hear heavenly music.*

Viola: *Dear lady—*

Olivia: *Let me talk, I ask you. After the last time you charmed me here, I sent a ring after you. By doing so, I mistreated my servant, you, and myself, I fear. I must accept your harsh criticism after I forced that on you in a shameful way, when you knew it was not yours. What must you think? Haven't you abused my defenseless honor? I have said enough for someone of your intelligence. Mourning clothing, not my bosom, hides my heart. So, let me hear what you have to say.*

Viola: *I pity you.*

Olivia: *That is a step towards love.*

120 VIOLA: No, not a grize; for 'tis a vulgar proof,
    That very oft we pity enemies.

OLIVIA: Why, then, methinks 'tis time to smile again.
    O, world, how apt the poor are to be proud!
    If one should be a prey, how much the better
125   To fall before the lion than the wolf! *[Clock strikes]*
    The clock upbraids me with the waste of time.
    Be not afraid, good youth, I will not have you:
    And yet, when wit and youth is come to harvest,
    Your were is alike to reap a proper man:
130   There lies your way, due west.

VIOLA: Then westward-ho! Grace and good disposition
    Attend your ladyship!
    You'll nothing, madam, to my lord by me?

OLIVIA: Stay:
135   I prithee, tell me what thou thinkest of me.

VIOLA: That you do think you are not what you are.

OLIVIA: If I think so, I think the same of you.

VIOLA: Then think you right: I am not what I am.

OLIVIA: I would you were as I would have you be!

140 VIOLA: Would it be better, madam, than I am?
    I wish it might, for now I am your fool.

OLIVIA: O, what a deal of scorn looks beautiful
    In the contempt and anger of his lip!
    A murderous guilt shows not itself more soon
145   Than love that would seem hid: love's night is noon.
    Cesario, by the roses of the spring,
    By maidhood, honour, truth and every thing,
    I love thee so, that, maugre all thy pride,

VIOLA: *No, not a step. I offer you the common proof that frequently we pity our enemies.*

OLIVIA: *Well then, I think it is time for me to be happy again. Oh, world, how easy it is for the poor to be proud! If someone must be a victim, it is so much better to be struck down by a lion than by a wolf!* [Clock strikes.] *The clock scolds me for wasting time. Do not be afraid, good young man, I do not want you. However, when you reach maturity, your wife, most likely, will have received a very handsome man. There is your out, to the west.*

VIOLA: *I am off to the west! May blessings and a happy life accompany you. You have no message for me to pass along to my lord, madam?*

OLIVIA: *Wait. Please, tell me what you think of me.*

VIOLA: *That you think you are something that you are not.*

OLIVIA: *If so, I think the same of you.*

VIOLA: *Then you are right. I am not what I am.*

OLIVIA: *I wish you were what I want you to be!*

VIOLA: *Would that be better, madam, than what I am now? I hope it would be, for you are making me look like a fool.*

OLIVIA: *Oh, how attractive he looks when he is angry! Feeling guilty for murdering someone does not reveal itself as quickly as love when you try to hide it. Love is easily revealed. Cesario, I swear by the roses of spring, maidenhood, honor, truth, and everything, I love you very much, despite all your pride. Neither cleverness nor reasoning can hide my passion. Do not misinterpret my confession, because you have given me no reason to*

111

Nor wit nor reason can my passion hide.
150   Do not extort thy reasons from this clause,
       For that I woo, thou therefore hast no cause,
       But rather reason thus with reason fetter,
       Love sought is good, but given unsought better.

       VIOLA: By innocence I swear, and by my youth
155   I have one heart, one bosom and one truth,
       And that no woman has; nor never none
       Shall mistress be of it, save I alone.
       And so adieu, good madam: never more
       Will I my master's tears to you deplore.

160   OLIVIA: Yet come again; for thou perhaps mayst move
       That heart, which now abhors, to like his love.

                                   [Exeunt]

SCENE 2
Olivia's house.

[Enter Sir Toby, Sir Andrew, and Fabian]

SIR ANDREW: No, faith, I'll not stay a jot longer.

SIR TOBY: Thy reason, dear venom, give thy reason.

FABIAN: You must needs yield your reason, Sir Andrew.

SIR ANDREW: Marry, I saw your niece do more favours to the
5   count's serving-man than ever she bestowed upon me; I saw
        't i' the orchard.

SIR TOBY: Did she see thee the while, old boy? tell me that.

SIR ANDREW: As plain as I see you now.

pursue you. Instead, consider that the love you seek is good, but when you receive love unsought, it is better.

VIOLA: *I swear by my innocence and youth that I have only one heart, one bosom, and one truth that I do not share with any woman. And no one will ever rule it except for me. So, goodbye, madam. I will never come again on behalf of my crying master.*

OLIVIA: *You should come again, because perhaps you can change my dislike for him into affection.*

[They exit.]

SCENE 2
Olivia's house.

[Enter Sir Toby, Sir Andrew, and Fabian.]

SIR ANDREW: *No, truly, I will not stay minute longer.*

SIR TOBY: *Your reason, dear grouch, give me you reason.*

FABIAN: *You must give us your reason, Sir Andrew.*

SIR ANDREW: *I swear, I saw your niece show more friendliness to the count's servant than she has ever shown me. I saw it in the garden.*

SIR TOBY: *Did she see you while you were there, old boy? Tell me that.*

SIR ANDREW: *As clearly as I see you now.*

FABIAN: This was a great argument of love in her toward you.

10   SIR ANDREW: 'Slight, will you make an ass o' me?

FABIAN: I will prove it legitimate, sir, upon the oaths of judgment
and reason.

SIR TOBY: And they have been grand-jury-men since before Noah
was a sailor.

15   FABIAN: She did show favour to the youth in your sight only to
exasperate you, to awake your dormouse valour, to put fire in
your heart and brimstone in your liver. You should then have
accosted her; and with some excellent jests, fire-new from the
mint, you should have banged the youth into dumbness. This
20   was looked for at your hand, and this was balked: the double
gilt of this opportunity you let time wash off, and you are
now sailed into the north of my lady's opinion; where you
will hang like an icicle on a Dutchman's beard, unless you do
redeem it by some laudable attempt either of valour or policy.

25   SIR ANDREW: An 't be any way, it must be with valour; for policy
I hate: I had as lief be a Brownist as a politician.

SIR TOBY: Why, then, build me thy fortunes upon the basis of
valour. Challenge me the count's youth to fight with him;
hurt him in eleven places: my niece shall take note of it; and
30   assure thyself, there is no love-broker in the world can more
prevail in man's commendation with woman than report of
valour.

FABIAN: There is no way but this, Sir Andrew.

SIR ANDREW: Will either of you bear me a challenge to him?

35   SIR TOBY: Go, write it in a martial hand; be curst and brief; it is
no matter how witty, so it be eloquent and fun of invention:

FABIAN: This is clear evidence of her love for you.

SIR ANDREW: In the name of God, are you making a fool of me?

FABIAN: I will prove it is true, sir, by using good sense and reason.

SIR TOBY: And they have been excellent judges since before Noah was a sailor.

FABIAN: She showed a liking for the young man in front of you only to infuriate you, wake up your sleeping bravery, put passion in your heart, and enflame your emotions. You should have attacked her then, and, with some excellent, brand new jokes, knock the young man into silence. This was expected from you and was missed. You missed this excellent opportunity and have now dropped in the lady's opinion, where you will hang like an icicle on a Dutchman's beard, unless you redeem yourself with a respectable deed of bravery or clever politics.

SIR ANDREW: If I have to do one of them, it will have to be a brave task, because I hate politics. I would rather be a religious fanatic than a politician.

SIR TOBY: Well then, build your luck upon the basis of your bravery. Challenge the count's servant to fight with you. Injure him in eleven places. My niece will be told about it. Assure yourself, telling a woman about a man's bravery is the most persuasive way in this world to make a match.

FABIAN: This is the only way, Sir Andrew.

SIR ANDREW: Will either of you take the challenge to him for me?

SIR TOBY: Go and write it in overbearing handwriting. Make it belligerent and short. It does not matter how witty it is, as long as it is well-written

115

40 taunt him with the licence of ink: if thou thou'st him some thrice, it shall not be amiss; and as many lies as will lie in thy sheet of paper, although the sheet were big enough for the bed of Ware in England, set 'em down: go, about it. Let there be gall enough in thy ink, though thou write with a goose-pen, no matter: about it.

SIR ANDREW: Where shall I find you?

SIR TOBY: We'll call thee at the cubiculo: go.
[Exit Sir Andrew]

45 FABIAN: This is a dear manikin to you, Sir Toby.

SIR TOBY: I have been dear to him, lad, some two thousand strong, or so.

FABIAN: We shall have a rare letter from him: but you'll not deliver't?

50 SIR TOBY: Never trust me, then; and by all means stir on the youth to an answer. I think oxen and wainropes cannot hale them together. For Andrew, if he were opened, and you find so much blood in his liver as will clog the foot of a flea, I'll eat the rest of the anatomy.

55 FABIAN: And his opposite, the youth, bears in his visage no great presage of cruelty.

[Enter Maria]

SIR TOBY: Look, where the youngest wren of nine comes.

MARIA: If you desire the spleen, and will laugh yourself into stitches, follow me. Yond gull Malvolio is turned heathen, a
60 very renegado; for there is no Christian, that means to be saved by believing rightly, can ever believe such impossible passages of grossness. He's in yellow stockings.

and creative. Taunt him with the advantages of writing. If you call him "thou" three or for times, it would not be inappropriate. Fill your sheet of paper with as many lies as will fit. eEven if the sheet is big enough for the huge bed of Ware in England, keep writing them. Go on, do it. Show plenty of boldness in your writing, even though you will be using a frilly pen to compose it. It does not matter. Go ahead, now.

SIR ANDREW: *Where will I find you?*

SIR TOBY: *We will come see you at your bedroom. Go.*
                                    [Exit Sir Andrew.]

FABIAN: *He is your sweet puppet, Sir Toby.*

SIR TOBY: *I have been valuable to him, lad, in the amount of two thousand pounds or so.*

FABIAN: *We will have an exceptional letter from him, but you are not going to deliver it?*

SIR TOBY: *Never trust me again if I do not, and I will do whatever it takes to make the young man answer the challenge. I do not think even oxen and cart-ropes could drag those two together. As for Andrew, if he were cut open and you found enough blood in his liver to clog the foot of a flea, I will eat the rest of him.*

FABIAN: *And his opponent, the young man, does not look vicious.*

[Enter Maria.]

SIR TOBY: *Look, here comes the little wren.*

MARIA: *If you want to laugh yourself into stitches, come with me. That fool, Malvolio, has turned against the church and deserted his religion, because no Christian could believe that such a ridiculous act would result in salvation. He is wearing yellow stockings.*

SIR TOBY: And cross-gartered?

MARIA: Most villanously; like a pedant that keeps a school i' the
65   church. I have dogged him, like his murderer. He does obey
every point of the letter that I dropped to betray him: he does
smile his face into more lines than is in the new map with
the augmentation of the Indies: you have not seen such a
thing as 'tis. I can hardly forbear hurling things at him. I
70   know my lady will strike him: if she do, he'll smile and take
't for a great favour.

SIR TOBY: Come, bring us, bring us where he is.

[Exeunt]

SCENE 3
A street.

[Enter Sebastian and Antonio]

SEBASTIAN: I would not by my will have troubled you;
      But, since you make your pleasure of your pains,
      I will no further chide you.

ANTONIO: I could not stay behind you: my desire,
5   More sharp than filed steel, did spur me forth;
      And not all love to see you, though so much
      As might have drawn one to a longer voyage,
      But jealousy what might befall your travel,
      Being skilless in these parts; which to a stranger,
10   Unguided and unfriended, often prove
      Rough and unhospitable: my willing love,
      The rather by these arguments of fear,
      Set forth in your pursuit.

SIR TOBY: And cross-gartered?

MARIA: Horribly, like a teacher who holds school in a church. I have followed him as if I were trying to kill him. He does everything that the letter, which I wrote to deceive him, says to do. His smile creates more lines on his face than the new map of the Indies. You have never seen anything like this. I can hardly stop myself from throwing things at him. I know my lady will strike him, and if she does, he will smile and think it is a compliment.

SIR TOBY: Bring us to him.

[They exit.]

SCENE 3
A street.

[Enter Sebastian and Antonio.]

SEBASTIAN: I would not have troubled you willingly, but since you seem to enjoy the trouble, I will no longer argue with you.

ANTONIO: I could not let you leave me behind. My desire, sharper than a knife, pushed me forward. I did not come just because I wanted to see you; although, I would travel farther to do that, but because I was concerned over what might happen to you, since you are unfamiliar to this place. A stranger, with no guide and no friend, may find this area cruel and unwelcoming. My great affection for you, along with these other fears, caused me to follow you.

SEBASTIAN: My kind Antonio,
15   I can no other answer make but thanks,
    And thanks; and ever…oft good turns
    Are shuffled off with such uncurrent pay:
    But, were my worth as is my conscience firm,
    You should find better dealing. What's to do?
20   Shall we go see the reliques of this town?

ANTONIO: To-morrow, sir: best first go see your lodging.

SEBASTIAN: I am not weary, and 'tis long to night:
    I pray you, let us satisfy our eyes
    With the memorials and the things of fame
25   That do renown this city.

ANTONIO: Would you 'ld pardon me;
    I do not without danger walk these streets:
    Once, in a sea-fight, 'gainst the count his galleys
    I did some service; of such note indeed,
30   That were I ta'en here it would scarce be answer'd.

SEBASTIAN: Belike you slew great number of his people.

ANTONIO: The offence is not of such a bloody nature;
    Albeit the quality of the time and quarrel
    Might well have given us bloody argument.
35   It might have since been answer'd in repaying
    What we took from them; which, for traffic's sake,
    Most of our city did: only myself stood out;
    For which, if I be lapsed in this place,
    I shall pay dear.

40 SEBASTIAN: Do not then walk too open.

ANTONIO: It doth not fit me. Hold, sir, here's my purse.
    In the south suburbs, at the Elephant,
    Is best to lodge: I will bespeak our diet,
    Whiles you beguile the time and feed your knowledge
45   With viewing of the town: there shall you have me.

SEBASTIAN: *My kind Antonio, I can say nothing else but thanks, and thanks, and more thanks. Usually good deeds are paid back with those useless thanks. If I had money to equal how much I am in debt to you, I would reward you better. What should we do? Go see the sights of this town?*

ANTONIO: *Tomorrow, sir. We had better find you a place to sleep first.*

SEBASTIAN: *I am not tired, and the night is young. Please, let us treat our eyes to the memorials and famous sights of this well-known city.*

ANTONIO: *If you will forgive me, it is dangerous for me to walk these streets. Once, in a sea battle against the count, I helped his enemies so much that, if I were caught, I would surely be killed.*

SEBASTIAN: *It seems you killed many of his people.*

ANTONIO: *What I did is not of such a gruesome nature, but the situation may have led to killing. It could be repaired by repaying what we took from them, which, for trade's sake, many already did. I am the only one who did not make amends, so, if I am caught here, I will pay dearly.*

SEBASTIAN: *Do not walk out in the open then.*

ANTONIO: *That does not suit me. Here, sir, take my money-pouch. In the south suburbs is the best place to lodge, at an inn called the Elephant. I will get us dinner while you spend the time sightseeing. You will find me at the inn.*

SEBASTIAN: Why I your purse?

ANTONIO: Haply your eye shall light upon some toy
    You have desire to purchase; and your store,
    I think, is not for idle markets, sir.

50   SEBASTIAN: I'll be your purse-bearer and leave you
    For an hour.

ANTONIO: To the Elephant.

SEBASTIAN: I do remember.

[Exeunt]

SCENE 4
Olivia's garden.

[Enter Olivia and Maria]

OLIVIA: I have sent after him: he says he'll come;
    How shall I feast him? what bestow of him?
    For youth is bought more oft than begg'd or borrow'd.
    I speak too loud.
5   Where is Malvolio? he is sad and civil,
    And suits well for a servant with my fortunes:
    Where is Malvolio?

MARIA: He's coming, madam; but in very strange manner. He is,
    sure, possessed, madam.

10 OLIVIA: Why, what's the matter? does he rave?

MARIA: No. madam, he does nothing but smile: your ladyship
    were best to have some guard about you, if he come; for,
    sure, the man is tainted in his wits.

SEBASTIAN: *Why should I take your money?*

ANTONIO: *You might see a souvenir that you want to buy, and I doubt you have enough money for frivolous things.*

SEBASTIAN: *I will take your money and leave you for an hour.*

ANTONIO: *Come to the Elephant.*

SEBASTIAN: *I will remember.*

[They exit.]

SCENE 4
Olivia's garden.

[Enter Olivia and Maria.]

OLIVIA: *I have invited him. He says he will come. What should I feed him? What gift should I give to him? Young men are more often won over by gifts than by begging or borrowing. I am speaking too loud. Where is Malvolio? He is serious and well-behaved, which is suitable for a servant of mine, given my current situation. Where is Malvolio?*

MARIA: *He is coming, madam, but he is acting very strangely. He is surely crazy, madam.*

OLIVIA: *Why? What is wrong? Is he raving?*

MARIA: *No, madam, he will not stop smiling. If he comes, you should be on guard, because surely the man has lost his mind.*

OLIVIA: Go call him hither. *[Exit Maria]* I am as mad as he,
15   If sad and merry madness equal be.

[Re-enter Maria, with Malvolio]
      How now, Malvolio!

MALVOLIO: Sweet lady, ho, ho.

OLIVIA: Smilest thou?
      I sent for thee upon a sad occasion.

20   MALVOLIO: Sad, lady! I could be sad: this does make some
      obstruction in the blood, this cross-gartering; but what of
      that? if it please the eye of one, it is with me as the very true
      sonnet is, 'Please one, and please all.'

OLIVIA: Why, how dost thou, man? what is the matter with thee?

25   MALVOLIO: Not black in my mind, though yellow in my legs. It
      did come to his hands, and commands shall be executed: I
      think we do know the sweet Roman hand.

OLIVIA: Wilt thou go to bed, Malvolio?

MALVOLIO: To bed! ay, sweet-heart, and I'll come to thee.

30   OLIVIA: God comfort thee! Why dost thou smile so and kiss thy
      hand so oft?

MARIA: How do you, Malvolio?

MALVOLIO: At your request! yes; nightingales answer daws.

MARIA: Why appear you with this ridiculous boldness before my
35   lady?

MALVOLIO: 'Be not afraid of greatness:' 'twas well writ.

OLIVIA: Go and tell him to come here. [Exit Maria.] I am as crazy as he is, if madness caused by sadness and madness caused by happiness are equal.
[Re-enter Maria, with Malvolio.]
Hello Malvolio!

MALVOLIO: Sweet lady, hello.

OLIVIA: Are you smiling? I asked you to come about a sad matter.

MALVOLIO: Sad, lady? I could be sad; this cross-gartering does obstruct the flow of blood, but who cares? If it is pleasing to one person, it is fine with me. Just as the very true poem says, "Please one, and please all."

OLIVIA: How are you doing, man? What is the matter with you?

MALVOLIO: I have no bad thoughts in my mind, although I am yellow in my legs. It did fall into his hands, and the commands will be followed. I think we know the sweet Roman handwriting.

OLIVIA: Would you like to go to bed, Malvolio?

MALVOLIO: To bed! Yes, sweetheart, go, and I will come to you.

OLIVIA: God help you! Why do you smile like that and kiss your hand so much?

MARIA: How are you, Malvolio?

MALVOLIO: Because you ask! Yes, nightingales answer crows.

MARIA: Why are you being ridiculously rude in front of my lady?

MALVOLIO: "Be not afraid of greatness." It was well written.

OLIVIA: What meanest thou by that, Malvolio?

MALVOLIO: 'Some are born great,'—

OLIVIA: Ha!

40 MALVOLIO: 'Some achieve greatness,'—

OLIVIA: What sayest thou?

MALVOLIO: 'And some have greatness thrust upon them.'

OLIVIA: Heaven restore thee!

MALVOLIO: 'Remember who commended thy yellow stocking s,'—

45 OLIVIA: Thy yellow stockings!

MALVOLIO: 'And wished to see thee cross-gartered.'

OLIVIA: Cross-gartered!

MALVOLIO: 'Go to thou art made, if thou desirest to be so;'—

50 OLIVIA: Am I made?

MALVOLIO: 'If not, let me see thee a servant still.'

OLIVIA: Why, this is very midsummer madness.

[Enter Servant]

SERVANT: Madam, the young gentleman of the Count Orsino's is
returned: I could hardly entreat him back: he attends your
55   ladyship's pleasure.

OLIVIA: *What do you mean by that, Malvolio?*

MALVOLIO: *"Some are born great—"*

OLIVIA: *Ha!*

MALVOLIO: *"Some achieve greatness—"*

OLIVIA: *What are you saying?*

MALVOLIO: *"And some have greatness thrust upon them."*

OLIVIA: *Heaven help you!*

MALVOLIO: *"Remember who complimented your yellow stockings—"*

OLIVIA: *Your yellow stockings!*

MALVOLIO: *"And wished to see you cross-gartered."*

OLIVIA: *Cross-gartered!*

MALVOLIO: *"Go ahead, you are made, if you want to be so—"*

OLIVIA: *Am I made?*

MALVOLIO: *"If not, let me see you act like a steward always."*

OLIVIA: *Well, this is midsummer madness, surely.*

[Enter Servant.]

SERVANT: *Madam, Count Orsino's young gentleman has come back. It was very difficult to convince him to come. He is waiting for your company.*

OLIVIA: I'll come to him. *[Exit Servant]* Good Maria, let this fellow be looked to. Where's my cousin Toby? Let some of my people have a special care of him: I would not have him miscarry for the half of my dowry.

[Exeunt Olivia and Maria]

60 MALVOLIO: O, ho! do you come near me now? no worse man than Sir Toby to look to me! This concurs directly with the letter: she sends him on purpose, that I may appear stubborn to him; for she incites me to that in the letter. 'Cast thy humble slough,' says she; 'be opposite with a kinsman, surly
65 with servants; let thy tongue tang with arguments of state; put thyself into the trick of singularity;' and consequently sets down the manner how; as, a sad face, a reverend carriage, a slow tongue, in the habit of some sir of note, and so forth. I have limed her; but it is Jove's doing, and Jove
70 make me thankful! And when she went away now, 'Let this fellow be looked to:' fellow! not Malvolio, nor after my degree, but fellow. Why, every thing adheres together, that
no dram of a scruple, no scruple of a scruple, no obstacle, no incredulous or unsafe circumstance—What can be said?
75 Nothing that can be can come between me and the full prospect of my hopes. Well, Jove, not I, is the doer of this, and he is to be thanked.

[Re-enter Maria, with Sir Toby Belch and Fabian]

SIR TOBY: Which way is he, in the name of sanctity? If all the devils of hell be drawn in little, and Legion himself possessed
80 him, yet I'll speak to him.

FABIAN: Here he is, here he is. How is't with you, sir? how is't with you, man?

MALVOLIO: Go off; I discard you: let me enjoy my private: go off.

MARIA: Lo, how hollow the fiend speaks within him! did not I
85 tell you? Sir Toby, my lady prays you to have a care of him.

128

OLIVIA: I will come to him. [Exit Servant.] Good Maria, have this fellow taken care of. Where is my Uncle Toby? Let some of my people take special care of him. I would not let him be hurt for half of my dowry.

[Exit Olivia and Maria.]

MALVOLIO: Oh my! Do you understand me now? There is no worse a man than Sir Toby to look after me! This agrees exactly with the letter. She is sending him on purpose, so I will act rudely to him. She told me to do that in the letter. "Shed your humble outer skin," she says; "be quarrelsome with a kinsman, surly with servants; let your tongue discuss important matters, put yourself into the practice of individualism." Therefore, she lays out the way to do it. For example, a sad face, a slow walk, a slow way of talking, clothes like a notable man, and so on. I have caught her, but it is God's work, and God, let me be thankful! And as she went away just now, "Have this fellow taken care of." Fellow! She did not say Malvolio, or call me by my rank, just fellow. Everything fits together, without one bit of doubt, not a bit of a bit of doubt. There is no obstacle, nothing stopping this—What can I say? Nothing could ever come between my hopes and me. Well, God is the one controlling this, and I thank Him.

[Re-enter Maria, with Sir Toby and Fabian.]

SIR TOBY: Where is he, in the name of what is holy? Even if all the devils of hell have united and Lucifer himself has possessed him, I will speak with him.

FABIAN: Here he is, here he is. How are you, sir? How are you, man?

MALVOLIO: Go away, I send you off. Let me enjoy my privacy. Go away.

MARIA: Look, how the fiend speaks from deep within him! Didn't I tell you? Sir Toby, my lady wants you to take care of him.

MALVOLIO: Ah, ha! does she so?

SIR TOBY: Go to, go to; peace, peace; we must deal gently with
him: let me alone. How do you, Malvolio? how is't with you?
What, man! defy the devil: consider, he's an enemy to
90   mankind.

MALVOLIO: Do you know what you say?

MARIA: La you, an you speak ill of the devil, how he takes it at
heart! Pray God, he be not bewitched!

FABIAN: Carry his water to the wise woman.

95   MARIA: Marry, and it shall be done to-morrow morning, if I live.
My lady would not lose him for more than I'll say.

MALVOLIO: How now, mistress!

MARIA: O Lord!

SIR TOBY: Prithee, hold thy peace; this is not the way: do you not
100   see you move him? let me alone with him.

FABIAN: No way but gentleness; gently, gently: the fiend is rough,
and will not be roughly used.

SIR TOBY: Why, how now, my bawcock! how dost thou, chuck?

MALVOLIO: Sir!

105   SIR TOBY: Ay, Biddy, come with me. What, man! 'tis not for
gravity to play at cherry-pit with Satan: hang him, foul
collier!

MARIA: Get him to say his prayers, good Sir Toby, get him to
pray.

MALVOLIO: *Oh, ha! Does she want that?*

SIR TOBY: *Come now, quiet, quiet. We must handle him carefully. Let me handle it. How are you doing, Malvolio? How are things with you? Come on, man! Defy the devil. Remember he is mankind's enemy.*

MALVOLIO: *Do you know what you are saying?*

MARIA: *See this, how he takes offense when you speak badly about the devil! Please God, do not let him be bewitched!*

FABIAN: *Take his water to the witch.*

MARIA: *By Mary, it will be done by tomorrow morning, as long as I am still living. My lady would not let him go for more money than I will say.*

MALVOLIO: *What, mistress!*

MARIA: *Oh Lord!*

SIR TOBY: *Please, keep quiet. This is not the way to handle him. Don't you see how you are upsetting him? Leave me to take care of him.*

FABIAN: *The only way is gentleness. Gently, gently. The fiend is violent and will not be treated brutally.*

SIR TOBY: *Well, hello, my fine fellow! How are you, chick?*

MALVOLIO: *Sir!*

SIR TOBY: *Yes, chicken, come with me. What, man! It is not right for a serious man like you to play games with Satan. Hang him, foul devil from hell!*

MARIA: *Get him to say his prayers, good Sir Toby. Get him to pray.*

110 MALVOLIO: My prayers, minx!

MARIA: No, I warrant you, he will not hear of godliness.

MALVOLIO: Go, hang yourselves all! you are idle shallow things: I
am not of your element: you shall know more hereafter.

[Exit]

SIR TOBY: Is't possible?

115 FABIAN: If this were played upon a stage now, I could condemn it
as an improbable fiction.

SIR TOBY: His very genius hath taken the infection of the device,
man.

MARIA: Nay, pursue him now, lest the device take air and taint.

120 FABIAN: Why, we shall make him mad indeed.

MARIA: The house will be the quieter.

SIR TOBY: Come, we'll have him in a dark room and bound. My
niece is already in the belief that he's mad: we may carry it
thus, for our pleasure and his penance, till our very pastime,
125 tired out of breath, prompt us to have mercy on him: at
which time we will bring the device to the bar and crown
thee for a finder of madmen. But see, but see.

[Enter Sir Andrew]

FABIAN: More matter for a May morning.

SIR ANDREW: Here's the challenge, read it: warrant there's vinegar
130 and pepper in 't.

FABIAN: Is 't so saucy?

MALVOLIO: *Say my prayers, minx!*

MARIA: *No, of course, he will not do anything godly.*

MALVOLIO: *All of you, go and hang yourselves! You are lazy, shallow people. I am not like you. You will know more later.* [He exits.]

SIR TOBY: *Is it possible?*

FABIAN: *If this were being acted out in a play right now, I would criticize it as being unrealistic.*

SIR TOBY: *He has totally fallen for our trick, man.*

MARIA: *Let us follow him, in case the joke gets a chance to go wrong.*

FABIAN: *Well, we will make him completely mad.*

MARIA: *The house will be much quieter.*

SIR TOBY: *Come on, we will have him committed to a lunatic asylum. My niece already thinks that he is crazy. We can make this happen, for our enjoyment and his punishment, until our worn out sport urges us to have mercy on him. At which time, we will wipe the slate clean and you will be respected for your ability to find madmen. However, look who is coming.*

[Enter Sir Andrew.]

FABIAN: *Another person to joke with.*

SIR ANDREW: *Here is the challenge, read it. I believe it is full of vinegar and pepper.*

FABIAN: *Is it that saucy?*

133

SIR ANDREW: Ay, is 't, I warrant him: do but read.

SIR TOBY: Give me. *[Reads]* 'Youth, whatsoever thou art, thou art
but a scurvy fellow.'

135 FABIAN: Good, and valiant.

SIR TOBY: *[Reads]* 'Wonder not, nor admire not in thy mind,
why I do call thee so, for I will show thee no reason for't.'

FABIAN: A good note; that keeps you from the blow of the law.

SIR TOBY: *[Reads]* 'Thou comest to the lady Olivia, and in my
140   sight she uses thee kindly: but thou liest in thy throat; that is
not the matter I challenge thee for.'

FABIAN: Very brief, and to exceeding good sense—less.

SIR TOBY: *[Reads]* 'I will waylay thee going home; where if it be thy
chance to kill me,'—

145 FABIAN: Good.

SIR TOBY: *[Reads]* 'Thou killest me like a rogue and a villain.'

FABIAN: Still you keep o' the windy side of the law: good.

SIR TOBY: *[Reads]* 'Fare thee well; and God have mercy upon one of
our souls! He may have mercy upon mine; but my hope is better,
150   and so look to thyself. Thy friend, as thou usest him, and thy
sworn enemy,
                    ANDREW AGUECHEEK.
If this letter move him not, his legs cannot: I'll give't him.

MARIA: You may have very fit occasion for't: he is now in some
155   commerce with my lady, and will by and by depart.

SIR TOBY: Go, Sir Andrew; scout me for him at the corner the

SIR ANDREW: *Yes, it is, definitely. Go ahead and read it.*

SIR TOBY: *Give it to me.* [Reads.] *Young man, whoever you are, you are a despicable fellow.*

FABIAN: *That is good and courageous.*

SIR TOBY: [Reads.] *Do not wonder or be surprised why I called you that, because I will not give you a reason.*

FABIAN: *A good touch. That keeps it legal.*

SIR TOBY: [Reads.] *You come to see the lady Olivia, and she treats you kindly in front of me. Nevertheless, you lie, and that is not the reason I am challenging you.*

FABIAN: *It is very to the point, and very good sense–less.*

SIR TOBY: [Reads.] *I will stop you on your way home, when, if by chance you are able to kill me—*

FABIAN: *Good.*

SIR TOBY: [Reads.] *You will kill me like a scoundrel and a villain.*

FABIAN: *Still you keep on the right side of the law. Good.*

SIR TOBY: [Reads.] *Goodbye and God have mercy upon one of our souls! He may have mercy on mine, but I think I have a better chance, so look yourself. Your friend, as you treated him, and your sworn enemy,*
> ANDREW AGUECHEEK.
If this letter does not get him moving, his legs will not be able to. I will give it to him.

MARIA: *You may have a good chance to do so. He is now talking with my lady and will soon leave.*

SIR TOBY: *Go, Sir Andrew. Watch him for me at the corner of the garden,*

orchard like a bum-baily: so soon as ever thou seest him,
draw; and, as thou drawest swear horrible; for it comes to
pass oft that a terrible oath, with a swaggering accent sharply
160   twanged off, gives manhood more approbation than ever
proof itself would have earned him. Away!

Sir Andrew: Nay, let me alone for swearing.   *[Exit]*

Sir Toby: Now will not I deliver his letter: for the behavior of the
young gentleman gives him out to be of good capacity and
165   breeding; his employment between his lord and my niece
confirms no less: therefore this letter, being so excellently
ignorant, will breed no terror in the youth: he will find it
comes from a clodpole. But, sir, I will deliver his challenge by
word of mouth; set upon Aguecheek a notable report of
170   valour; and drive the gentleman, as I know his youth will
aptly receive it, into a most hideous opinion of his rage, skill,
fury and impetuosity. This will so fright them both that they
will kill one another by the look, like cockatrices.

[Re-enter Olivia, with Viola]

Fabian: Here he comes with your niece: give them way till he
175   take leave, and presently after him.

Sir Toby: I will meditate the while upon some horrid message
for a challenge.   *[Exeunt Sir Toby, Fabian, and Maria]*

Olivia: I have said too much unto a heart of stone
And laid mine honour too unchary out:
180   There's something in me that reproves my fault;
But such a headstrong potent fault it is,
That it but mocks reproof.

Viola: With the same 'havior that your passion bears
Goes on my master's grief.

185 Olivia: Here, wear this jewel for me, 'tis my picture;

136

like an officer. As soon as you see him, draw your sword, and as you draw, swear horribly. Very often, a terrible oath said with great self-confidence gives a man a better reputation than actual fighting would have given him. Go now!

SIR ANDREW: *Leave the swearing to me.* [He exits.]

SIR TOBY: *I will not deliver this letter now, because the behavior of that young man shows he is able to take care of himself and is from a good family. His job as a messenger between his lord and my niece confirms this. Therefore, this letter that is so incredibly ignorant will not scare the youth. He will see that it comes from a blockhead. But, sir, I will deliver the challenge by speaking to the young man. I will tell him Aguecheek is very brave and will give the gentleman, since I know he will believe it, as young as he is, a false idea of his rage, skill, fury, and recklessness. This will make them both so frightened that they will kill one another just by looking at each other, like cockatrices.*

[Re-enter Olivia, with Viola.]

FABIAN: *Here he comes with your niece. Let them talk until he leaves, and then follow him.*

SIR TOBY: *In the meantime, I will come up with some terrifying presentation of the challenge.*   [Exit Sir Toby, Fabian, and Maria.]

OLIVIA: *I have said too much to a cold heart. I have laid out my honor too carelessly. A part of me disapproves of my mistake, but it is a fault that is so headstrong that it does not care about the disapproval.*

VIOLA: *My master's grief has that same characteristic as your passion.*

OLIVIA: *Here, wear this locket for me. It has my picture. Do not refuse to*

Refuse it not; it hath no tongue to vex you;
And I beseech you come again to-morrow.
What shall you ask of me that I'll deny,
That honour saved may upon asking give?

190 VIOLA: Nothing but this; your true love for my master.

OLIVIA: How with mine honour may I give him that
    Which I have given to you?

VIOLA: I will acquit you.

OLIVIA: Well, come again to-morrow: fare thee well:
195   A fiend like thee might bear my soul to hell. *[Exit]*

[Re-enter Sir Toby and Fabian]

SIR TOBY: Gentleman, God save thee.

VIOLA: And you, sir.

SIR TOBY: That defence thou hast, betake thee to't: of what
nature the wrongs are thou hast done him, I know not; but
200 thy intercepter, full of despite, bloody as the hunter, attends
thee at the orchard-end: dismount thy tuck, be yare in thy
preparation, for thy assailant is quick, skilful and deadly.

VIOLA: You mistake, sir; I am sure no man hath any quarrel to
me: my remembrance is very free and clear from any image of
205 offence done to any man.

SIR TOBY: You'll find it otherwise, I assure you: therefore, if you
hold your life at any price, betake you to your guard; for
your opposite hath in him what youth, strength, skill and
wrath can furnish man withal.

210 VIOLA: I pray you, sir, what is he?

take it. It cannot speak to you and annoy you. I beg you to come again tomorrow. What can you ask of me that I will not give, as long as it is honorable?

VIOLA: I will ask for nothing, except for your true love for my master.

OLIVIA: How can I honorably give him what I have already given to you?

VIOLA: I will free you.

OLIVIA: Well, come again tomorrow. Goodbye. A fiend like you could take my soul to hell.　　　　　　[She exits.]

[Re-enter Sir Toby and Fabian.]

SIR TOBY: Gentleman, God bless you.

VIOLA: And you, sir.

SIR TOBY: Get your defense ready. What wrong you have done to him, I do not know, but your challenger, full of anger, bloody as a hunter, waits for you at the garden. Draw your sword, be quiet in your preparation, for your assailant is quick, skillful, and deadly.

VIOLA: You are mistaken, sir. I am sure no man has a problem with me. My memory is free and clear from any wrong I may have done to any man.

SIR TOBY: You will discover that is not true, I promise you. Therefore, if you value your life, be on guard because your opponent has in him the gifts of youth, strength, skill, and wrath.

VIOLA: Please, sir. Who is he?

SIR TOBY: He is knight, dubbed with unhatched rapier and on carpet consideration; but he is a devil in private brawl: souls and bodies hath he divorced three; and his incensement at this moment is so implacable, that satisfaction can be none
215 but by pangs of death and sepulchre. Hob, nob, is his word; give't or take't.

VIOLA: I will return again into the house and desire some conduct of the lady. I am no fighter. I have heard of some kind of men that put quarrels purposely on others, to taste
220 their valour: belike this is a man of that quirk.

SIR TOBY: Sir, no; his indignation derives itself out of a very competent injury: therefore, get you on and give him his desire. Back you shall not to the house, unless you undertake that with me which with as much safety you might answer
225 him: therefore, on, or strip your sword stark naked; for meddle you must, that's certain, or forswear to wear iron about you.

VIOLA: This is as uncivil as strange. I beseech you, do me this courteous office, as to know of the knight what my offence to
230 him is: it is something of my negligence, nothing of my purpose.

SIR TOBY: I will do so. Signior Fabian, stay you by this gentleman till my return.   [Exit]

VIOLA: Pray you, sir, do you know of this matter?

235 FABIAN: I know the knight is incensed against you, even to a mortal arbitrement; but nothing of the circumstance more.

VIOLA: I beseech you, what manner of man is he?

FABIAN: Nothing of that wonderful promise, to read him by his form, as you are like to find him in the proof of his valour.
240 He is, indeed, sir, the most skilful, bloody and fatal opposite

SIR TOBY: *He is a knight, dubbed with an unused sword as he knelt on a carpet. However, he is a devil in a one-on-one fight. He has killed three people, and his anger is so relentless right now, that only killing someone and burying him will satisfy it. "Hit or miss" is his saying, take it or leave it.*

VIOLA: *I will go back into the house and talk with the lady. I am not a fighter. I have heard of men who purposely start fights with others, just to test their bravery. I believe this is a man who does that.*

SIR TOBY: *No, sir! He has a very real reason for being angry. Therefore, you had better go ahead and give him what he wants. You will not go back into the house, unless you fight me, which would be just as dangerous as fighting him. Therefore, go, or draw your sword now, because you must fight, that is for sure, or stop carrying a weapon with you.*

VIOLA: *This is as rude as it is strange. I beg you, do me this favor: have the knight tell me how I have offended him. It is something I did by accident, not on purpose.*

SIR TOBY: *I will do that. Mister Fabian, wait with this gentleman until I come back.* [He exits.]

VIOLA: *Please, sir. Do you know anything about this?*

FABIAN: *I know the knight is furious at you, to the point of wanting to fight you to the death, but I do not know why.*

VIOLA: *I ask you, what kind of man is he?*

FABIAN: *If you only look at him, you cannot guess how he is while fighting. He is, truly, sir, the most skillful, bloody, and deadly opponent you could*

that you could possibly have found in any part of Illyria. Will
you walk towards him? I will make your peace with him if I
can.

VIOLA: I shall be much bound to you for't: I am one that had
245   rather go with sir priest than sir knight: I care not who
knows so much of my mettle.   *[Exeunt]*

[Re-enter Sir Toby, with Sir Andrew]

SIR TOBY: Why, man, he's a very devil; I have not seen such a
firago. I had a pass with him, rapier, scabbard and all, and he
gives me the stuck in with such a mortal motion, that it is
250   inevitable; and on the answer, he pays you as surely as your
feet hit the ground they step on. They say he has been fencer
to the Sophy.

SIR ANDREW: Pox on 't, I'll not meddle with him.

SIR TOBY: Ay, but he will not now be pacified: Fabian can scarce
255   hold him yonder.

SIR ANDREW: Plague on 't, an I thought he had been valiant and
so cunning in fence, I'ld have seen him damned ere I'ld have
challenged him. Let him let the matter slip, and I'll give him
my horse, grey Capilet.

260 SIR TOBY: I'll make the motion: stand here, make a good show
on 't: this shall end without the perdition of souls.
[Aside] Marry, I'll ride your horse as well as I ride you.

[Re-enter Fabian and Viola]
[To Fabian] I have his horse to take up the quarrel: I have
persuaded him the youth's a devil.

265 FABIAN: He is as horribly conceited of him; and pants and looks
pale, as if a bear were at his heels.

have found anywhere in Illyria. Are you willing to approach him? I will
make your peace with him, if I can.

VIOLA: *I will be very indebted to you for it. I am one who would rather get*
married than fight. I do not care who knows that about my personality.

[They exit. Re-enter Sir Toby with Sir Andrew.]

SIR TOBY: *Well, man, he is like a devil. I have never seen such a hothead. I*
had an encounter with him, sword, sheath, and all. He thrust at me with
such a deadly accuracy that it was sure to strike. On the next thrust, he
strikes you as definitely as your feet hit the ground they walk on. They
say he has been a fencer for the Shah of Persia.

SIR ANDREW: *Curse it. I will not fight him.*

SIR TOBY: *Yes, but he will not be appeased now. Fabian can hardly hold him*
back.

SIR ANDREW: *Damn it. If I had thought he were so brave and so skillful at*
fencing, I would have seen him damned before I'd have challenged him.
Tell him I will let this matter go, and I will give him my horse, Gray
Capilet.

SIR TOBY: *I will give him the offer. Stay here, do your best, and this will end*
without a death. [Aside.] *By Mary, I'll ride your horse as well as I take*
your for a ride.
[Re-enter Fabian and Viola.]
[To Fabian.] *I have his horse to settle the argument. I have convinced*
him the young man is a devil.

FABIAN: *He is as terrified of the knight. He breathes hard and looks pale, as*
if a bear were chasing him.

Sir Toby: *[To Viola]* There's no remedy, sir; he will fight with you
for's oath sake: marry, he hath better bethought him of his
quarrel, and he finds that now scarce to be worth talking of:
270   therefore draw, for the supportance of his vow; he protests he
will not hurt you.

Viola: *[Aside]* Pray God defend me! A little thing would make
me tell them how much I lack of a man.

Fabian: Give ground, if you see him furious.

275   Sir Toby: Come, Sir Andrew, there's no remedy; the gentleman
will, for his honour's sake, have one bout with you; he
cannot by the duello avoid it: but he has promised me, as he
is a gentleman and a soldier, he will not hurt you. Come on;
to't.

280   Sir Andrew: Pray God, he keep his oath!

Viola: I do assure you, 'tis against my will.   *[They draw]*

[Enter Antonio]

Antonio: Put up your sword. If this young gentleman
Have done offence, I take the fault on me:
If you offend him, I for him defy you.

285   Sir Toby: You, sir! why, what are you?

Antonio: One, sir, that for his love dares yet do more
Than you have heard him brag to you he will.

Sir Toby: Nay, if you be an undertaker, I am for you.
                                     [They draw]

[Enter Officers]

Fabian: O good Sir Toby, hold! here come the officers.

144

SIR TOBY: [To Viola.] *There is no resolving this, sir. He will fight with you, because he has taken an oath to do so. By Mary, he has had second thoughts about the duel, and he knows now that it was not worth talking about. Therefore, draw your sword, and defend yourself against his oath. He has promised he will not hurt you.*

VIOLA: [Aside.] *Please, God, defend me! Something small could push me to tell them I am not a man.*

FABIAN: *Back off, if you see that he is furious.*

SIR TOBY: *Come here, Sir Andrew. There is no resolving this. The gentleman will, for the sake of his honor, have one session with you. He cannot, by the code of dueling, avoid it. However, he has promised me, as a gentleman and soldier, that he will not hurt you. Come on, get to it.*

SIR ANDREW: *Please, God. Let him keep his promise!*

VIOLA: *I assure you, I do not want to do this.* [They draw their swords.]

[Enter Antonio.]

ANTONIO: *Put away your sword. If this young man has offended you, I will take the blame for him. If you offended him, I despise you on his behalf.*

SIR TOBY: *You, sir! Why, who are you?*

ANTONIO: *I am one, sir, who, for my love, will dare to do more than you have heard me say I will do.*

SIR TOBY: *Well, if you are a person who will take on this task, I am the man who will fight you.* [They draw their swords.]

[Enter Officers.]

FABIAN: *Oh, good Sir Toby, wait! Here come the officers.*

290   SIR TOBY: I'll be with you anon.

VIOLA: Pray, sir, put your sword up, if you please.

SIR ANDREW: Marry, will I, sir; and, for that I promised you, I'll
    be as good as my word: he will bear you easily and reins well.

FIRST OFFICER: This is the man; do thy office.

295   SECOND OFFICER: Antonio, I arrest thee at the suit of Count
    Orsino.

ANTONIO: You do mistake me, sir.

FIRST OFFICER: No, sir, no jot; I know your favour well,
    Though now you have no sea-cap on your head.
300   Take him away: he knows I know him well.

ANTONIO: I must obey. *[To Viola]* This comes with seeking you:
    But there's no remedy; I shall answer it.
    What will you do, now my necessity
    Makes me to ask you for my purse? It grieves me
305   Much more for what I cannot do for you
    Than what befalls myself. You stand amazed;
    But be of comfort.

SECOND OFFICER: Come, sir, away.

ANTONIO: I must entreat of you some of that money.

310   VIOLA: What money, sir?
    For the fair kindness you have show'd me here,
    And, part, being prompted by your present trouble,
    Out of my lean and low ability
    I'll lend you something: my having is not much;
315   I'll make division of my present with you:
    Hold, there's half my coffer.

SIR TOBY: *I will be with you in a minute.*

VIOLA: *Please, sir. Put away your sword, please.*

SIR ANDREW: *By Mary, I will, sir. As for what I promised you, I will honor my word. Gray Capilet will carry you comfortably and is easy to control.*

FIRST OFFICERICER: *This is the man. Carry out your orders.*

SECOND OFFICER: *Antonio, I arrest you at the request of Count Orsino.*

ANTONIO: *You are mistaken, sir.*

FIRST OFFICER: *No, sir, no way. I know what you look like very well, although now you do not have a sailor's hat on your head. Take him away. He knows I know him well.*

ANTONIO: *I must submit. [To Viola.] This happened because I was looking for you, but there is no way to fix it. I will face it. How will you get by, now that I must ask you for my purse? I am much more upset about what I cannot do for you now, than for what is happening to me. You look surprised, but do not be upset.*

SECOND OFFICER: *Come on, sir. Let's go.*

ANTONIO: *I must ask you for some of that money.*

VIOLA: *What money, sir? For the excellent kindness you have shown me here, and because of your current problem, I will lend you something from my limited funds. What I have is not a lot, but I will divide it in half with you. Here, there is half of my money.*

147

ANTONIO: Will you deny me now?
    Is 't possible that my deserts to you
    Can lack persuasion? Do not tempt my misery,
320   Lest that it make me so unsound a man
    As to upbraid you with those kindnesses
    That I have done for you.

VIOLA: I know of none;
    Nor know I you by voice or any feature:
325   I hate ingratitude more in a man
    Than lying, vainness, babbling, drunkenness,
    Or any taint of vice whose strong corruption
    Inhabits our frail blood.

ANTONIO: O heavens themselves!

330 SECOND OFFICER: Come, sir, I pray you, go.

ANTONIO: Let me speak a little. This youth that you see here
    I snatch'd one half out of the jaws of death,
    Relieved him with such sanctity of love,
    And to his image, which methought did promise
335   Most venerable worth, did I devotion.

FIRST OFFICER: What's that to us? The time goes by: away!

ANTONIO: But O how vile an idol proves this god
    Thou hast, Sebastian, done good feature shame.
    In nature there's no blemish but the mind;
340   None can be call'd deform'd but the unkind:
    Virtue is beauty, but the beauteous evil
    Are empty trunks o'erflourish'd by the devil.

FIRST OFFICER: The man grows mad: away with him! Come,
    come, sir.

345 ANTONIO: Lead me on.   *[Exit with Officers]*

ANTONIO: Will you reject me now? Is it possible that my good deeds I have done for you do not matter? Do not test my misery, because it may make me so upset that I will severely criticize you by naming those kindnesses that I have done for you.

VIOLA: I do not know of any, nor do I know you by the sound of your voice or your face. I hate ingratitude more in a man than lying boastfulness, babbling drunkenness, or any other vices that corrupt mankind.

ANTONIO: Oh, my heavens!

SECOND OFFICER: Come on sir, please, let's go.

ANTONIO: Let me say something. This young man that you see here, I pulled from the jaws of death. I cared for him with sacred love, and worshipped his image, which I thought was completely deserving.

FIRST OFFICER: Why does that matter to us? The time is passing. Away!

ANTONIO: What a horrible idol you have proven to be! You have, Sebastian, brought shame upon your features. In nature, there is no imperfection worse than the mind. None, except for the cruel, can be called deformed. Virtue is beautiful, but the beautiful ones who are evil are empty trunks, richly decorated by the devil.

FIRST OFFICER: The man is going crazy, take him away. Come on, come on, sir.

ANTONIO: Lead me on. [He exits with the Officers.]

149

VIOLA: Methinks his words do from such passion fly,
    That he believes himself: so do not I.
    Prove true, imagination, O, prove true,
    That I, dear brother, be now ta'en for you!

350   SIR TOBY: Come hither, knight; come hither, Fabian: we'll
    whisper o'er a couplet or two of most sage saws.

VIOLA: He named Sebastian: I my brother know
    Yet living in my glass; even such and so
    In favour was my brother, and he went
355   Still in this fashion, colour, ornament,
    For him I imitate: O, if it prove,
    Tempests are kind and salt waves fresh in love.   *[Exit]*

SIR TOBY: A very dishonest paltry boy, and more a coward than
    a hare: his dishonesty appears in leaving his friend here in
360   necessity and denying him; and for his cowardship, ask
    Fabian.

FABIAN: A coward, a most devout coward, religious in it.

SIR ANDREW: 'Slid, I'll after him again and beat him.

SIR TOBY: Do; cuff him soundly, but never draw thy sword.

365   SIR ANDREW: An I do not,—

FABIAN: Come, let's see the event.

SIR TOBY: I dare lay any money 'twill be nothing yet.
                                [Exeunt]

VIOLA: *By the passionate way he is speaking, I think he believes what he is saying. However, I do not. Please let my thoughts turn out to be true that I have been mistaken for you, dear brother!*

SIR TOBY: *Come here, knight. Come here, Fabian. We will trade a few wise words.*

VIOLA: *He named Sebastian. I know my brother is still living when I look in my mirror. My brother looked exactly like me, and he dressed in this way, in this color and design. I know, because I am imitating him. Oh, if it is true, then storms are kind, and waves are loving!* [She exits.]

SIR TOBY: *A very dishonest and despicable boy, and more of a coward than a rabbit. His dishonesty was shown when he left his friend in need and denied that he knew him. Ask Fabian about his cowardice.*

FABIAN: *A coward, a most devoted coward. It is like a religion to him.*

SIR ANDREW: *By God, I will go after him again and assault him.*

SIR TOBY: *Go ahead. Beat him up well, but do not draw your sword.*

SIR ANDREW: *And if I do not—* [He exits.]

FABIAN: *Come on, let's watch this.*

SIR TOBY: *I will bet that nothing will come of this.*
[They exit.]

151

ACT IV

SCENE 1
Before Olivia's house.

[Enter Sebastian and Clown]

CLOWN: Will you make me believe that I am not sent for you?

SEBASTIAN: Go to, go to, thou art a foolish fellow:
Let me be clear of thee.

CLOWN: Well held out, i' faith! No, I do not know you; nor I am
5   not sent to you by my lady, to bid you come speak with her;
nor your name is not Master Cesario; nor this is not my nose
neither. Nothing that is so is so.

SEBASTIAN: I prithee, vent thy folly somewhere else:
Thou know'st not me.

10   CLOWN: Vent my folly! he has heard that word of some great
man and now applies it to a fool. Vent my folly! I am afraid
this great lubber, the world, will prove a cockney. I prithee
now, ungird thy strangeness and tell me what I shall vent to
my lady: shall I vent to her that thou art coming?

15   SEBASTIAN: I prithee, foolish Greek, depart from me:
There's money for thee: if you tarry longer,
I shall give worse payment.

ACT IV

SCENE 1
Before Olivia's house.

[Enter Sebastian and Feste, a Clown.]

CLOWN: *Are you trying to make me believe that I was not sent to find you?*

SEBASTIAN: *Come on, come on, you are a foolish man. Please leave me alone.*

CLOWN: *You are keeping the pretending up well, I swear! No, I do not know you, nor was I sent to you by my lady to ask you to come speak with her. Your name is not Master Cesario, and this is not my nose, either. Nothing is what I say it is.*

SEBASTIAN: *I beg you, vent your joking somewhere else. You do not know me.*

CLOWN: *Vent my joking! You have heard that word from some great man and now you apply it to a fool. Vent my joking! I am afraid this blundering fool, the world, will turn out to be a sissy. I ask you now, stop being aloof and tell what I should vent to my lady. Should I vent to her that you are coming?*

SEBASTIAN: *I ask you, foolish man, get away from me. Here is money for you. If you stay longer, I will give you a worse payment.*

CLOWN: By my troth, thou hast an open hand. These wise men that give fools money get themselves a good report—after fourteen years' purchase.

20

[Enter Sir Andrew, Sir Toby, and Fabian]

SIR ANDREW: Now, sir, have I met you again? there's for you.

SEBASTIAN: Why, there's for thee, and there, and there. Are all the people mad?

SIR TOBY: Hold, sir, or I'll throw your dagger o'er the house.

25 CLOWN: This will I tell my lady straight: I would not be in some of your coats for two pence.   *[Exit]*

SIR TOBY: Come on, sir; hold.

SIR ANDREW: Nay, let him alone: I'll go another way to work with him; I'll have an action of battery against him, if there 30 be any law in Illyria: though I struck him first, yet it's no matter for that.

SEBASTIAN: Let go thy hand.

SIR TOBY: Come, sir, I will not let you go. Come, my young soldier, put up your iron: you are well fleshed; come on.

35 SEBASTIAN: I will be free from thee. What wouldst thou now? If thou darest tempt me further, draw thy sword.

SIR TOBY: What, what? Nay, then I must have an ounce or two of this malapert blood from you.

[Enter Olivia]

OLIVIA: Hold, Toby; on thy life I charge thee, hold!

CLOWN: I swear, you are very generous. Wise men that give fools money earn a good reputation–after fourteen years of payment.

[Enter Sir Andrew, Sir Toby, and Fabian.]

SIR ANDREW: Now, sir, do we meet again? This is for you.

SEBASTIAN: Well this is for you, and that, and that. Are all you people crazy?

SIR TOBY: Stop, sir, or I will throw your sword over the house.

CLOWN: I will go tell my lady about this right away. I would not take your places for two pennies.   [He exits.]

SIR TOBY: Come on, sir, stop.

SIR ANDREW: No, leave him alone. I will go after him another way. I will sue him for battery, if there are any laws in Illyria. Although, I did strike him first, but that does not matter.

SEBASTIAN: Let go of me.

SIR TOBY: Come on, sir. I will not let you go. Come on, my young soldier, put away your sword. You have fighting experience, come on.

SEBASTIAN: I will be free from you. What do you want now? If you dare to push me further, draw your sword.

SIR TOBY: What, what? Well, then I must have an ounce or two of your audacious blood.

[Enter Olivia.]

OLIVIA: Stop, Toby! On your life, I command you to stop!

40   Sɪʀ Tᴏʙʏ: Madam!

Oʟɪᴠɪᴀ: Will it be ever thus? Ungracious wretch,
     Fit for the mountains and the barbarous caves,
     Where manners ne'er were preach'd! out of my sight!
     Be not offended, dear Cesario.
45   Rudesby, be gone!
                [Exeunt Sir Toby, Sir Andrew, and Fabian]
     I prithee, gentle friend,
     Let thy fair wisdom, not thy passion, sway
     In this uncivil and thou unjust extent
50   Against thy peace. Go with me to my house,
     And hear thou there how many fruitless pranks
     This ruffian hath botch'd up, that thou thereby
     Mayst smile at this: thou shalt not choose but go:
     Do not deny. Beshrew his soul for me,
55   He started one poor heart of mine in thee.

Sᴇʙᴀsᴛɪᴀɴ: What relish is in this? how runs the stream?
     Or I am mad, or else this is a dream:
     Let fancy still my sense in Lethe steep;
     If it be thus to dream, still let me sleep!

60   Oʟɪᴠɪᴀ: Nay, come, I prithee; would thou'ldst be ruled by me!

Sᴇʙᴀsᴛɪᴀɴ: Madam, I will.

Oʟɪᴠɪᴀ: O, say so, and so be!   *[Exeunt]*

SIR TOBY: *Madam!*

OLIVIA: *Will it always be like this? Unmannerly scoundrel, you are only fit for mountains and uncivilized caves, where no manners were ever taught! Get out of my sight! Do not be offended, dear Cesario. Boor, get out of here! [Exit Sir Toby, Sir Andrew, and Fabian.] May I ask you, gentle friend, let your common sense, not your anger, take over in how you respond to this rude and unjust attack on your peace. Come with me to my house and you can hear about how many pointless pranks this ruffian has ruined. That way maybe you can smile at this. You must come. Do not deny me. Curse his soul; he gave a shock to my part of your heart.*

SEBASTIAN: *What is she suggesting? What is going on? Either I am crazy, or this is a dream. Let me stay unaware. If I am dreaming, let me keep sleeping!*

OLIVIA: *Now, come with me, please. I wish that you would do as I say!*

SEBASTIAN: *Madam, I will.*

OLIVIA: *Oh, just say that, and let it be!*   [They exit.]

SCENE 2
Olivia's house.

[Enter Maria and Clown]

MARIA: Nay, I prithee, put on this gown and this beard; make
    him believe thou art Sir Topas the curate: do it quickly; I'll
    call Sir Toby the whilst.   *[Exit]*

CLOWN: Well, I'll put it on, and I will dissemble myself in 't; and
5   I would I were the first that ever dissembled in such a gown.
    I am not tall enough to become the function well, nor lean
    enough to be thought a good student; but to be said an
    honest man and a good housekeeper goes as fairly as to say a
    careful man and a great scholar. The competitors enter.

[Enter Sir Toby and Maria]

10   SIR TOBY: Jove bless thee, master Parson.

CLOWN: Bonos dies, Sir Toby: for, as the old hermit of Prague,
    that never saw pen and ink, very wittily said to a niece of
    King Gorboduc, 'That that is is;' so I, being Master Parson,
    am Master Parson; for, what is 'that' but 'that,' and 'is' but 'is'?

15   SIR TOBY: To him, Sir Topas.

CLOWN: What, ho, I say! peace in this prison!

SIR TOBY: The knave counterfeits well; a good knave.

MALVOLIO: *[Within]* Who calls there?

CLOWN: Sir Topas the curate, who comes to visit Malvolio the
20   lunatic.

MALVOLIO: Sir Topas, Sir Topas, good Sir Topas, go to my lady.

SCENE 2
Olivia's house.

[Enter Maria and Feste, a Clown.]

MARIA: *Now, I ask you, put on this robe and this beard. Make him believe that you are Sir Topas, the priest. Do it quickly. I will call Sir Toby in the meantime.*   [She exits.]

CLOWN: *Well, I will put it on, and I will disguise myself in it. I wish I were the first that had ever used the robe as a disguise. I am not respectable looking enough to pretend to be him well. I am not lean enough to be thought of as a good student, either, but to be called an honest man and a good host is as good as being named a cautious man and a great scholar. The partners enter.*

[Enter Sir Toby.]

SIR TOBY: *God bless you, master Parson.*

CLOWN: *Good day, Sir Toby. As the old hermit of Prague, that never saw pen and ink, said very wittily to his niece about King Gorboduc, "That that is is." So, I, being master Parson, am master Parson, because what is meant by "that" but "that," and "is" but "is"?*

SIR TOBY: *Go to him, Sir Topas.*

CLOWN: *Hello in there, I say! Peace in this prison!*

SIR TOBY: *The fellow acts the part well. He is a good fellow.*

MALVOLIO: [Within] *Who is there?*

CLOWN: *Sir Topas, the priest, who has come to visit Malvolio, the lunatic.*

MALVOLIO: *Sir Topas, Sir Topas, good Sir Topas, go to my lady.*

CLOWN: Out, hyperbolical fiend! how vexest thou this man! talkest thou nothing but of ladies?

SIR TOBY: Well said, Master Parson.

25 MALVOLIO: Sir Topas, never was man thus wronged: good Sir Topas, do not think I am mad: they have laid me here in hideous darkness.

CLOWN: Fie, thou dishonest Satan! I call thee by the most modest terms; for I am one of those gentle ones that will use
30 the devil himself with courtesy: sayest thou that house is dark?

MALVOLIO: As hell, Sir Topas.

CLOWN: Why it hath bay windows transparent as barricadoes, and the clearstores toward the south north are as lustrous as
35 ebony; and yet complainest thou of obstruction?

MALVOLIO: I am not mad, Sir Topas: I say to you, this house is dark.

CLOWN: Madman, thou errest: I say, there is no darkness but ignorance; in which thou art more puzzled than the
40 Egyptians in their fog.

MALVOLIO: I say, this house is as dark as ignorance, though ignorance were as dark as hell; and I say, there was never man thus abused. I am no more mad than you are: make the trial of it in any constant question.

45 CLOWN: What is the opinion of Pythagoras concerning wild fowl?

MALVOLIO: That the soul of our grandam might haply inhabit a bird.

CLOWN: I cast you out, outrageous fiend! How you are tormenting this man! Do you talk about nothing but ladies?

SIR TOBY: Well said, master Parson.

MALVOLIO: Sir Topas, never was a man treated as wrongly as I am being. Good Sir Topas, do not think I am mad. They have laid me here in hideous darkness.

CLOWN: Shame on you, dishonest Satan! I use reserved language about you, because I am one of those gentle people that will treat the devil himself with courtesy. Did you say that it is dark in there?

MALVOLIO: Dark as hell, Sir Topas.

CLOWN: Why, it has bay windows, transparent as barricades, and the upper windows toward the north south are as bright as ebony. Yet, you complain of darkness?

MALVOLIO: I am not crazy, Sir Topas. I swear to you, this place is dark.

CLOWN: Madman, you are wrong. I am telling you, there is no darkness but ignorance, and you are more wrapped up in it than the Egyptians were in the biblical fog.

MALVOLIO: I am telling you, this place is as dark as ignorance, if ignorance were as dark as hell. And I say, there was never a man who was so mistreated as I am being. I am no crazier than you are. Test my sanity by asking me any certain questions.

CLOWN: What does Pythagoras think about wild birds?

MALVOLIO: That the soul of our grandmother might live within a bird.

CLOWN: What thinkest thou of his opinion?

50 MALVOLIO: I think nobly of the soul, and no way approve his
    opinion.

CLOWN: Fare thee well. Remain thou still in darkness: thou shalt
    hold the opinion of Pythagoras ere I will allow of thy wits,
    and fear to kill a woodcock, lest thou dispossess the soul of
55 thy grandam. Fare thee well.

MALVOLIO: Sir Topas, Sir Topas!

SIR TOBY: My most exquisite Sir Topas!

CLOWN: Nay, I am for all waters.

MARIA: Thou mightst have done this without thy beard and
60 gown: he sees thee not.

SIR TOBY: To him in thine own voice, and bring me word how
    thou findest him: I would we were well rid of this knavery. If
    he may be conveniently delivered, I would he were, for I am
    now so far in offence with my niece that I cannot pursue
65 with any safety this sport to the upshot. Come by and by to
    my chamber.   [Exeunt Sir Toby and Maria]

CLOWN: [Singing] 'Hey, Robin, jolly Robin,
          Tell me how thy lady does.'

MALVOLIO: Fool!

70 CLOWN: 'My lady is unkind, perdy.'

MALVOLIO: Fool!

CLOWN: 'Alas, why is she so?'

MALVOLIO: Fool, I say!

CLOWN: What do you think of his opinion?

MALVOLIO: I think of the soul as noble and do not agree at all with his opinion.

CLOWN: Goodbye. Stay in the darkness. You will agree with Pythagoras before I believe that you are sane. Be afraid of killing a woodcock, because it might dislocate the soul of your grandmother. Goodbye.

MALVOLIO: Sir Topas, Sir Topas!

SIR TOBY: My most exquisite Sir Topas!

CLOWN: Oh, I am very flexible.

MARIA: You could have done this without your beard and robe. He did not see you.

SIR TOBY: Go talk to him as yourself, and let me know how he is doing. I wish we were done with this trickery. If he can be appropriately set free, I wish he would be, because I have now offended my niece so much that I cannot safely continue with this trick to its end. Come to my room soon.
[Exit Sir Toby and Maria.]

CLOWN: [Singing] Hey, Robin, jolly Robin,
        Tell me how thy lady does.

MALVOLIO: Fool—

CLOWN: My lady is unkind, indeed.

MALVOLIO: Fool—

CLOWN: Alas, why is she so?

MALVOLIO: Fool, I say—

CLOWN: 'She loves another'—Who calls, ha?

75 MALVOLIO: Good fool, as ever thou wilt deserve well at my hand,
help me to a candle, and pen, ink and paper: as I am a
gentleman, I will live to be thankful to thee for't.

CLOWN: Master Malvolio?

MALVOLIO: Ay, good fool.

80 CLOWN: Alas, sir, how fell you besides your five wits?

MALVOLIO: Fool, there was never a man so notoriously abused: I
am as well in my wits, fool, as thou art.

CLOWN: But as well? then you are mad indeed, if you be no
better in your wits than a fool.

85 MALVOLIO: They have here propertied me; keep me in darkness,
send ministers to me, asses, and do all they can to face me
out of my wits.

CLOWN: Advise you what you say; the minister is here. Malvolio,
Malvolio, thy wits the heavens restore! endeavour thyself to
90 sleep, and leave thy vain bibble babble.

MALVOLIO: Sir Topas!

CLOWN: Maintain no words with him, good fellow. Who, I, sir?
not I, sir. God be wi' you, good Sir Topas. Merry, amen. I will,
sir, I will.

95 MALVOLIO: Fool, fool, fool, I say!

CLOWN: Alas, sir, be patient. What say you sir? I am shent for
speaking to you.

CLOWN: *She loves another. Who is calling for me?*

MALVOLIO: *Good fool, if you ever want to be treated well by me, help me get a candle, pen, ink, and paper. As I am a gentleman, I will live to be thankful to you for it.*

CLOWN: *Master Malvolio!*

MALVOLIO: *Yes, good fool.*

CLOWN: *Oh, sir, how did you lose your mind?*

MALVOLIO: *Fool, there never was a man as abused as I am being. I am as sane, fool, as you are.*

CLOWN: *Only as sane? Then you are crazy, indeed, if you are no saner than a fool is.*

MALVOLIO: *They have imprisoned me here, kept me in darkness, sent ministers to me, the idiots, and done all they can to drive me crazy.*

CLOWN: *Watch what you say, the minister is here. Malvolio, Malvolio, may the heavens restore your sanity! Attempt to go to sleep, and stop your worthless chatter.*

MALVOLIO: *Sir Topas—*

CLOWN: *Do not talk with him, good fellow. Who, I, sir? Not I, sir. God be with you, good Sir Topas. By Mary, amen. I will, sir, I will.*

MALVOLIO: *Fool, fool, fool, I say—*

CLOWN: *Please, sir, be patient. What did you say, sir? I am reprimanded for speaking to you.*

MALVOLIO: Good fool, help me to some light and some paper: I tell thee, I am as well in my wits as any man in Illyria.

100 CLOWN: Well-a-day that you were, sir

MALVOLIO: By this hand, I am. Good fool, some ink, paper and light; and convey what I will set down to my lady: it shall advantage thee more than ever the bearing of letter did.

CLOWN: I will help you to't. But tell me true, are you not mad
105   indeed? or do you but counterfeit?

MALVOLIO: Believe me, I am not; I tell thee true.

CLOWN: Nay, I'll ne'er believe a madman till I see his brains. I will fetch you light and paper and ink.

MALVOLIO: Fool, I'll requite it in the highest degree: I prithee, be
110   gone.

CLOWN: *[Singing]*
        I am gone, sir,
          And anon, sir,
        I'll be with you again,
115   In a trice,
          Like to the old Vice,
        Your need to sustain;
        Who, with dagger of lath,
        In his rage and his wrath,
120   Cries, ah, ha! to the devil:
        Like a mad lad,
        Pare thy nails, dad;
          Adieu, good man devil.   *[Exit]*

MALVOLIO: *Good fool, help me get some light and some paper. I tell you, I am as sane as any man in Illyria is.*

CLOWN: *I wish that you were, sir!*

MALVOLIO: *I swear that I am. Good fool, some ink, paper, and light. And take what I have written to my lady. It will benefit you more than the carrying of any letter ever has.*

CLOWN: *I will help you get those things. But tell me the truth, are you really not mad? Or are you only pretending?*

MALVOLIO: *Believe me, I am not. I am telling you the truth.*

CLOWN: *No, I will never believe a madman until I see his brains. I will get you the light, paper, and ink.*

MALVOLIO: *Fool, I will repay you tremendously. I beg you, go.*

CLOWN: [Singing]
>*I am gone, sir,*
>>*And anon, sir,*
>*I'll be with you again,*
>>*In a trice,*
>>*Like to the old vice,*
>*Your need to sustain;*
>*Who, with dagger of lath,*
>*In his rage and his wrath,*
>>*Cries, ah, ha! to the devil:*
>*Like a mad lad,*
>*Pare thy nails, dad:*
>>*Adieu, goodman devil.*   [He exits.]

SCENE 3
Olivia's garden.

[Enter Sebastian]

SEBASTIAN: This is the air; that is the glorious sun;
　　　　This pearl she gave me, I do feel't and see't;
　　　　And though 'tis wonder that enwraps me thus,
　　　　Yet 'tis not madness. Where's Antonio, then?
5　　　I could not find him at the Elephant:
　　　　Yet there he was; and there I found this credit,
　　　　That he did range the town to seek me out.
　　　　His counsel now might do me golden service;
　　　　For though my soul disputes well with my sense,
10　　That this may be some error, but no madness,
　　　　Yet doth this accident and flood of fortune
　　　　So far exceed all instance, all discourse,
　　　　That I am ready to distrust mine eyes
　　　　And wrangle with my reason that persuades me
15　　To any other trust but that I am mad
　　　　Or else the lady's mad; yet, if 'twere so,
　　　　She could not sway her house, command her followers,
　　　　Take and give back affairs and their dispatch
　　　　With such a smooth, discreet and stable bearing
20　　As I perceive she does: there's something in 't
　　　　That is deceiveable. But here the lady comes.

[Enter Olivia and Priest]

OLIVIA: Blame not this haste of mine. If you mean well,
　　　　Now go with me and with this holy man
　　　　Into the chantry by: there, before him,
25　　And underneath that consecrated roof,
　　　　Plight me the full assurance of your faith;
　　　　That my most jealous and too doubtful soul
　　　　May live at peace. He shall conceal it
　　　　Whiles you are willing it shall come to note,
30　　What time we will our celebration keep
　　　　According to my birth. What do you say?

[Enter Sebastian.]

SEBASTIAN: *This is the air. That is the glorious sun. This pearl she gave me;*
I feel it and see it. Although I am enveloped in wonder, this is not mad-
ness. Where is Antonio, then? I could not find him at the Elephant, but
he had been there. I was told he had been searching for me around the
town. His advice could be very useful right now. My conscience is argu-
ing skillfully with my common sense that this all may be a mistake, but
not madness. Yet, this accident and string of good luck so far exceeds any
examples I have ever heard, that I am ready to disbelieve my eyes and
argue with my mind when it tries to convince me that the only explana-
tion for this is that I am crazy, or that the lady is crazy. However, if that
were true, she would not be able to control her house, rule her followers,
and discuss and take care of business affairs in the smooth, prudent, and
stable way that I have seen her. There is something in this situation that
is deceptive. Here comes the lady.

[Enter Olivia and Priest.]

OLIVIA: *Do not blame me for being in a rush. If your intentions are good,*
come with this holy man and me into the nearby church. There, before
him and underneath that sacred roof, swear to me your wedding vows,
so my jealous and distrustful soul can live in peace. He will keep this a
secret until you want to reveal it, and, at that time, we will have a cel-
ebration more appropriate to my position. What do you say?

SEBASTIAN: I'll follow this good man, and go with you;
    And, having sworn truth, ever will be true.

OLIVIA: Then lead the way, good father; and heavens so shine,
35   That they may fairly note this act of mine!

                                        [Exeunt]

SEBASTIAN: *I will follow this good man, and go with you. After having sworn my vows to you, I will always be true to you.*

OLIVIA: *Then lead the way, good father, and may the heavens shine down approvingly on what I am doing!*

[They go.]

ACT V

SCENE 1
Before Olivia's house.

[Enter Clown and Fabian]

FABIAN: Now, as thou lovest me, let me see his letter.

CLOWN: Good Master Fabian, grant me another request.

FABIAN: Any thing.

CLOWN: Do not desire to see this letter.

5 FABIAN: This is, to give a dog, and in recompense desire my dog
again.

[Enter Duke Orsino, Viola, Curio, and Lords]

DUKE ORSINO: Belong you to the Lady Olivia, friends?

CLOWN: Ay, sir; we are some of her trappings.

DUKE ORSINO: I know thee well; how dost thou, my good fellow?

10 CLOWN: Truly, sir, the better for my foes and the worse for my
friends.

DUKE ORSINO: Just the contrary; the better for thy friends.

ACT V

SCENE 1
Before Olivia's house.

[Enter Feste, a Clown and Fabian.]

FABIAN: *Now, since we are friends, let me see his letter.*

CLOWN: *Good Master Fabian, allow me to make another request.*

FABIAN: *Anything.*

CLOWN: *Do not ask to see this letter.*

FABIAN: *This is like giving me a dog and then, in return, asking me to give you back the dog.*

[Enter Duke, Viola, Curio, and Lords.]

DUKE: *Are you Lady Olivia's servants, friends?*

CLOWN: *Yes, sir. We are some of her ornaments.*

DUKE: *I know you well. How are you, my good fellow?*

CLOWN: *Truly, sir, I am better for having my enemies and worse for having my friends.*

DUKE: *On the contrary, better for having your friends.*

CLOWN: No, sir, the worse.

DUKE ORSINO: How can that be?

15 CLOWN: Marry, sir, they praise me and make an ass of me; now
my foes tell me plainly I am an ass: so that by my foes, sir I
profit in the knowledge of myself, and by my friends, I am
abused: so that, conclusions to be as kisses, if your four
negatives make your two affirmatives why then, the worse for
20 my friends and the better for my foes.

DUKE ORSINO: Why, this is excellent.

CLOWN: By my troth, sir, no; though it please you to be one of
my friends.

DUKE ORSINO: Thou shalt not be the worse for me: there's gold.

25 CLOWN: But that it would be double-dealing, sir, I would you
could make it another.

DUKE ORSINO: O, you give me ill counsel.

CLOWN: Put your grace in your pocket, sir, for this once, and let
your flesh and blood obey it.

30 DUKE ORSINO: Well, I will be so much a sinner, to be a
double-dealer: there's another.

CLOWN: Primo, secundo, tertio, is a good play; and the old
saying is, the third pays for all: the triplex, sir, is a good
tripping measure; or the bells of Saint Bennet, sir, may put
35 you in mind; one, two, three.

DUKE ORSINO: You can fool no more money out of me at this
throw: if you will let your lady know I am here to speak
with her, and bring her along with you, it may awake my
bounty further.

CLOWN: No, sir, the worse.

DUKE: How can that be true?

CLOWN: By Mary, sir, they compliment me and make a fool of me. Now, my enemies tell me forthrightly that I am a fool. Therefore, by my enemies, sir, I benefit from knowing more about myself, and by my friends, I am abused. So, if conclusions are like kisses, if four negatives make two positives, then I am the worse for having my friends, and the better for having my foes.

DUKE: Well, that is excellent.

CLOWN: I swear, I am not, sir. Although it is kind of you to be one of my friends.

DUKE: You will not be worse off because of me. There is some gold.

CLOWN: But then it would be trickery, sir. I wish you could give me another.

DUKE: Oh, you give me poor advice.

CLOWN: Put your pride in your pocket for just this once, sir, and obey your instincts.

DUKE: Well, I will sin by being a trickster. There is another.

CLOWN: One, two, three, is a good showing, and the old saying goes: the third is lucky. A triple beat, sir, is good for dancing. The bells of Saint Bennet, sir, may make you remember. One, two, three.

DUKE: You cannot fool me out of any more money right now. However, if you tell your lady that I am here and wish to speak with her, and then bring her back, my generosity may wake up again.

40　CLOWN: Marry, sir, lullaby to your bounty till I come again. I go,
　　　　sir; but I would not have you to think that my desire of
　　　　having is the sin of covetousness: but, as you say, sir, let your
　　　　bounty take a nap, I will awake it anon.　　　*[Exit]*

　　VIOLA: Here comes the man, sir, that did rescue me.

　　[Enter Antonio and Officers]

45　DUKE ORSINO: That face of his I do remember well;
　　　　Yet, when I saw it last, it was besmear'd
　　　　As black as Vulcan in the smoke of war:
　　　　A bawbling vessel was he captain of,
　　　　For shallow draught and bulk unprizable;
50　　　With which such scathful grapple did he make
　　　　With the most noble bottom of our fleet,
　　　　That very envy and the tongue of loss
　　　　Cried fame and honour on him. What's the matter?

　　FIRST OFFICER: Orsino, this is that Antonio
55　　　That took the Phoenix and her fraught from Candy;
　　　　And this is he that did the Tiger board,
　　　　When your young nephew Titus lost his leg:
　　　　Here in the streets, desperate of shame and state,
　　　　In private brabble did we apprehend him.

60　VIOLA: He did me kindness, sir, drew on my side;
　　　　But in conclusion put strange speech upon me:
　　　　I know not what 'twas but distraction.

　　DUKE ORSINO: Notable pirate! thou salt-water thief!
　　　　What foolish boldness brought thee to their mercies,
65　　　Whom thou, in terms so bloody and so dear,
　　　　Hast made thine enemies?

　　ANTONIO: Orsino, noble sir,
　　　　Be pleased that I shake off these names you give me:
　　　　Antonio never yet was thief or pirate,

CLOWN: By Mary, sir, sing a lullaby to your generosity until I come back. I am going, sir, but I do not want you to think that my desire for money is the sin of materialism. However, as you said, sir, let your generosity take a nap. I will awaken it soon.   [He exits.]

VIOLA: Here comes the man, sir that rescued me.

[Enter Antonio and Officers.]

DUKE: I remember his face well, but when I last saw it, it was smeared black from the smoke of war. He was the captain of an unimportant boat, which was not worth a lot because it was small and unable to sail deep into the water. He fought so fiercely with the best ship of our fleet that those who had good reason to hate him and complained about their loss, declared his fame and honor. What is happening with him?

FIRST OFFICER: Orsino, this is the Antonio, who seized the Phoenix and its cargo from Crete. He is also the man who got onto the Tiger when your young nephew, Titus, lost his leg. We found him in the street engaged in an argument, recklessly disregarding his wanted status.

VIOLA: He did me a favor, sir, drawing his sword to fight on my side. However, afterwards he said some strange things to me. I do not know what he meant and assumed he was insane.

DUKE: Famous pirate! You are the ocean thief! What reckless behavior brought you to the mercy of the enemies you have made by bloodshed and killing?

ANTONIO: Orsino, noble sir, please let me argue against the names you call me. I have never been a thief or a pirate, although I confess I am considered your enemy for good reasons. Witchcraft brought me here. I saved

70   Though I confess, on base and ground enough,
      Orsino's enemy. A witchcraft drew me hither:
      That most ingrateful boy there by your side,
      From the rude sea's enraged and foamy mouth
      Did I redeem; a wreck past hope he was:
75   His life I gave him and did thereto add
      My love, without retention or restraint,
      All his in dedication; for his sake
      Did I expose myself, pure for his love,
      Into the danger of this adverse town;
80   Drew to defend him when he was beset:
      Where being apprehended, his false cunning,
      Not meaning to partake with me in danger,
      Taught him to face me out of his acquaintance,
      And grew a twenty years removed thing
85   While one would wink; denied me mine own purse,
      Which I had recommended to his use
      Not half an hour before.

VIOLA: How can this be?

DUKE ORSINO: When came he to this town?

90   ANTONIO: To-day, my lord; and for three months before,
      No interim, not a minute's vacancy,
      Both day and night did we keep company.

[Enter Olivia and Attendants]

DUKE ORSINO: Here comes the countess: now heaven walks on
          earth.
95   But for thee, fellow; fellow, thy words are madness:
      Three months this youth hath tended upon me;
      But more of that anon. Take him aside.

OLIVIA: What would my lord, but that he may not have,
      Wherein Olivia may seem serviceable?
100   Cesario, you do not keep promise with me.

that terribly ungrateful boy by your side from the stormy and dangerous sea. He was a hopeless wreck. I gave him his life and added my unrestrained love devoted to his needs. For his sake and because of my love for him, I exposed myself to the danger of this adverse town. I came to defend him when he was under attack. When I was captured, he used skillful deceit to deny boldly that he knew me, so that he would not end up in danger with me. In the blink of an eye, he turned into someone who had not seen me for twenty years. He even would not give me my own money, which I had lent to him less than a half an hour before.

VIOLA: How can this be true?

DUKE: When did he come to this town?

ANTONIO: Today, my lord, and he constantly spent both day and night with me, without even a minute away, for the past three months.

[Enter Olivia and Attendants.]

DUKE: Here comes the countess. Now heaven walks on earth. As for you, fellow, your words are madness. This young man has been my servant for the past three months. However, we will talk more about that later. Take him aside.

OLIVIA: What do you want from me, my lord, other than what I cannot give you? Cesario, you are not keeping your promise to me.

VIOLA: Madam!

DUKE ORSINO: Gracious Olivia,—

OLIVIA: What do you say, Cesario? Good my lord,—

VIOLA: My lord would speak; my duty hushes me.

105 OLIVIA: If it be aught to the old tune, my lord,
It is as fat and fulsome to mine ear
As howling after music.

DUKE ORSINO: Still so cruel?

OLIVIA: Still so constant, lord.

110 DUKE ORSINO: What, to perverseness? you uncivil lady,
To whose ingrate and unauspicious altars
My soul the faithfull'st offerings hath breathed out
That e'er devotion tender'd! What shall I do?

OLIVIA: Even what it please my lord, that shall become him.

115 DUKE ORSINO: Why should I not, had I the heart to do it,
Like to the Egyptian thief at point of death,
Kill what I love?—a savage jealousy
That sometimes savours nobly. But hear me this:
Since you to non-regardance cast my faith,
120 And that I partly know the instrument
That screws me from my true place in your favour,
Live you the marble-breasted tyrant still;
But this your minion, whom I know you love,
And whom, by heaven I swear, I tender dearly,
125 Him will I tear out of that cruel eye,
Where he sits crowned in his master's spite.
Come, boy, with me; my thoughts are ripe in mischief:
I'll sacrifice the lamb that I do love,
To spite a raven's heart within a dove.

VIOLA: *Madam!*

DUKE: *Gracious Olivia—*

OLIVIA: *What are you saying, Cesario? Excuse me, my lord—*

VIOLA: *My lord wants to speak, and my duty to him silences me.*

OLIVIA: *If you are singing the same tune, my lord, it is as dull and nauseating to my ears as haring howling after music.*

DUKE: *Still so cruel?*

OLIVIA: *Still so steadfast, lord.*

DUKE: *To what, stubbornness? You rude lady, to your ungrateful and discouraging altar my soul has offered the most faithful words that were ever spoken in devotion! What shall I do?*

OLIVIA: *Whatever my lord wants to do, that will fit him.*

DUKE: *Why shouldn't I, if I had the heart to do it, kill what I love, like the Egyptian thief facing death? That was a savage jealousy that was somewhat noble. But listen to me say this: since you throw away my love as if it means nothing to you, and I suspect I know what has removed me from my rightful place in your affections, keep being a hardhearted tyrant. But this favorite of yours, whom I know you love, and whom I care for dearly, I will tear him away from your cruel eye, where he is crowned, despite his master. Come, boy, with me. My thoughts are full of evil deeds. I will sacrifice the lamb that I love, to spite the raven's heart that hides in the dove.*

130 VIOLA: And I, most jocund, apt and willingly,
　　　　To do you rest, a thousand deaths would die.

OLIVIA: Where goes Cesario?

VIOLA: After him I love
　　　　More than I love these eyes, more than my life,
135　　More, by all mores, than e'er I shall love wife.
　　　　If I do feign, you witnesses above
　　　　Punish my life for tainting of my love!

OLIVIA: Ay me, detested! how am I beguiled!

VIOLA: Who does beguile you? who does do you wrong?

140 OLIVIA: Hast thou forgot thyself? is it so long?
　　　　Call forth the holy father.

DUKE ORSINO: Come, away!

OLIVIA: Whither, my lord? Cesario, husband, stay.

DUKE ORSINO: Husband!

145 OLIVIA: Ay, husband: can he that deny?

DUKE ORSINO: Her husband, sirrah!

VIOLA: No, my lord, not I.

OLIVIA: Alas, it is the baseness of thy fear
　　　　That makes thee strangle thy propriety:
150　　Fear not, Cesario; take thy fortunes up;
　　　　Be that thou know'st thou art, and then thou art
　　　　As great as that thou fear'st.

[Enter Priest]
　　　　O, welcome, father!

VIOLA: And I, most cheerfully, readily, and willingly, would die a thousand deaths if it would satisfy you.

OLIVIA: Where is Cesario going?

VIOLA: After him that I love more than I love these eyes, more than my life, more, by far, than I'll ever love a wife. If I am lying, may those watching above, punish me for disgracing the one I love!

OLIVIA: Oh, I am renounced! How I have been tricked!

VIOLA: Who tricks you? Who does you wrong?

OLIVIA: Have you forgotten who you are? Has it been so long? Tell the holy father to come here.

DUKE: Come, let us go!

OLIVIA: Where, my lord? Cesario, husband, stay.

DUKE: Husband!

OLIVIA: Yes, husband. Can he deny it?

DUKE: Her husband, sir!

VIOLA: No, my lord, not me.

OLIVIA: Oh, it is your cowardly fear that is making you deny who you are. Do not be afraid, Cesario. Embrace your good luck. Be what you know you are, and then you will be as great as the man you fear.

[Enter Priest.] Oh, welcome, father! Father, I ask you, as you are a very respected man, to tell, although we intended to keep a secret what is

Father, I charge thee, by thy reverence,
155 Here to unfold, though lately we intended
To keep in darkness what occasion now
Reveals before 'tis ripe, what thou dost know
Hath newly pass'd between this youth and me.

PRIEST: A contract of eternal bond of love,
160 Confirm'd by mutual joinder of your hands,
Attested by the holy close of lips,
Strengthen'd by interchangement of your rings;
And all the ceremony of this compact
Seal'd in my function, by my testimony:
165 Since when, my watch hath told me, toward my grave
I have travell'd but two hours.

DUKE ORSINO: O thou dissembling cub! what wilt thou be
When time hath sow'd a grizzle on thy case?
Or will not else thy craft so quickly grow,
170 That thine own trip shall be thine overthrow?
Farewell, and take her; but direct thy feet
Where thou and I henceforth may never meet.

VIOLA: My lord, I do protest—

OLIVIA: O, do not swear!
175 Hold little faith, though thou hast too much fear.

[Enter Sir Andrew]

SIR ANDREW: For the love of God, a surgeon! Send one presently
to Sir Toby.

OLIVIA: What's the matter?

SIR ANDREW: He has broke my head across and has given Sir
180 Toby a bloody coxcomb too: for the love of God, your help! I
had rather than forty pound I were at home.

now being revealed, what you know has recently happened between this young man and me.

PRIEST: *A vow of eternal love, which was confirmed by the joining of your hands, proven by your holy kiss, and strengthened by the exchanging of your rings. All the ceremony of these vows were made official by me as a chaplain and witness. My watch tells me it has been two hours since this took place.*

DUKE: *Oh, you deceitful cub! What will you be like when time has given you gray hair? Or will your craft not grow so quickly that you will ruin yourself? Goodbye, and take her, but go where you and I will never meet again.*

VIOLA: *My lord, I do swear—*

OLIVIA: *Oh, do not swear! Keep a little trustworthiness, although you are so fearful.*

[Enter Sir Andrew.]

SIR ANDREW: *For the love of God, a surgeon! Send one immediately to Sir Toby.*

OLIVIA: *What is wrong?*

SIR ANDREW: *He has busted my head open and given Sir Toby a bloody head, too. For the love of God, we need your help! I would give forty pounds to be home.*

OLIVIA: Who has done this, Sir Andrew?

SIR ANDREW: The count's gentleman, one Cesario: we took him
for a coward, but he's the very devil incardinate.

185   DUKE ORSINO: My gentleman, Cesario?

SIR ANDREW: 'Od's lifelings, here he is! You broke my head for
nothing; and that that I did, I was set on to do't by Sir Toby.

VIOLA: Why do you speak to me? I never hurt you:
You drew your sword upon me without cause;
190 .   But I bespoke you fair, and hurt you not.

SIR ANDREW: If a bloody coxcomb be a hurt, you have hurt me: I
think you set nothing by a bloody coxcomb.

[Enter Sir Toby and Clown]
Here comes Sir Toby halting; you shall hear more: but if he
had not been in drink, he would have tickled you othergates
195   than he did.

DUKE ORSINO: How now, gentleman! how is't with you?

SIR TOBY: That's all one: has hurt me, and there's the end on't.
Sot, didst see Dick surgeon, sot?

CLOWN: O, he's drunk, Sir Toby, an hour agone; his eyes were set
200   at eight i' the morning.

SIR TOBY: Then he's a rogue, and a passy measures panyn: I hate
a drunken rogue.

OLIVIA: Away with him! Who hath made this havoc with them?

SIR ANDREW: I'll help you, Sir Toby, because well be dressed
205   together.

OLIVIA: Who has done this, Sir Andrew?

SIR ANDREW: The count's gentleman, Cesario. We thought he was a coward, but he is the devil in the flesh.

DUKE: My gentleman, Cesario?

SIR ANDREW: Good God, he is here! You broke open my head for no reason. What I did, Sir Toby made me do.

VIOLA: Why are you speaking to me? I never hurt you. You drew your sword on me for no reason, but I spoke nicely to you and did not hurt you.

SIR ANDREW: If a bloody head is a hurt, you have hurt me. I think a bloody head means nothing to you.

[Enter Sir Toby and Feste, a Clown.] Here comes Sir Toby, limping. You will hear more, but if he had not been drinking, he would have dealt with you better than he did.

DUKE: Hello, gentlemen! How are you?

SIR TOBY: It is all the same. He has hurt me, and there is the end of it. Idiot, did you see Dick the surgeon, idiot?

CLOWN: Oh, he has been drunk for an hour, Sir Toby. His eyes were glassy at eight in the morning.

SIR TOBY: Then he is a scoundrel and a stumbling idiot. I hate a drunken scoundrel.

OLIVIA: Take him away! Who has caused this trouble with them?

SIR ANDREW: I will help you, Sir, Toby, because we will have our wounds treated together.

SIR TOBY: Will you help? an ass-head and a coxcomb and a knave, a thin-faced knave, a gull!

OLIVIA: Get him to bed, and let his hurt be look'd to.
[Exeunt Clown, Fabian, Sir Toby, and Sir Andrew]

[Enter Sebastian]

SEBASTIAN: I am sorry, madam, I have hurt your kinsman:
210   But, had it been the brother of my blood,
I must have done no less with wit and safety.
You throw a strange regard upon me, and by that
I do perceive it hath offended you:
Pardon me, sweet one, even for the vows
215   We made each other but so late ago.

DUKE ORSINO: One face, one voice, one habit, and two persons,
A natural perspective, that is and is not!

SEBASTIAN: Antonio, O my dear Antonio!
How have the hours rack'd and tortured me,
220   Since I have lost thee!

ANTONIO: Sebastian are you?

SEBASTIAN: Fear'st thou that, Antonio?

ANTONIO: How have you made division of yourself?
An apple, cleft in two, is not more twin
225   Than these two creatures. Which is Sebastian?

OLIVIA: Most wonderful!

SEBASTIAN: Do I stand there? I never had a brother;
Nor can there be that deity in my nature,
Of here and every where. I had a sister,
230   Whom the blind waves and surges have devour'd.
Of charity, what kin are you to me?
What countryman? what name? what parentage?

SIR TOBY: You will help me? A blockhead, an idiot, and a rascal, a thin-faced rascal, a fool!

OLIVIA: Get him to bed and treat his injuries.
            [Exit Feste, a Clown, Fabian, Sir Toby, and Sir Andrew.]

[Enter Sebastian.]

SEBASTIAN: I am sorry that I have hurt your uncle, madam. However, even if it had been my own brother, I would have done the same thing to protect my safety. You are looking at me strangely, and it tells me that I have offended you. Forgive me, sweet one, because of the vows we recently made to each other.

DUKE: One face, one voice, one way of dressing, and two people. A living optical illusion that is and is not!

SEBASTIAN: Antonio, oh my dear Antonio! I have been tortured by the hours since I lost you!

ANTONIO: Are you Sebastian?

SEBASTIAN: Do you doubt that, Antonio?

ANTONIO: How have you split yourself in half? An apple cut in half is as similar as these two people. Which is Sebastian?

OLIVIA: It is amazing!

SEBASTIAN: Am I standing over there? I never had a brother, and I do not have any godlike powers that allow me to be two places at once. I had a sister, but she was drowned by the ocean. Please tell me, how are you related to me? What country are you from? What is your name? Who are your parents?

VIOLA: Of Messaline: Sebastian was my father;
Such a Sebastian was my brother too,
235   So went he suited to his watery tomb:
If spirits can assume both form and suit
You come to fright us.

SEBASTIAN: A spirit I am indeed;
But am in that dimension grossly clad
240   Which from the womb I did participate.
Were you a woman, as the rest goes even,
I should my tears let fall upon your cheek,
And say 'Thrice-welcome, drowned Viola!'

VIOLA: My father had a mole upon his brow.

245 SEBASTIAN: And so had mine.

VIOLA: And died that day when Viola from her birth
Had number'd thirteen years.

SEBASTIAN: O, that record is lively in my soul!
He finished indeed his mortal act
250   That day that made my sister thirteen years.

VIOLA: If nothing lets to make us happy both
But this my masculine usurp'd attire,
Do not embrace me till each circumstance
Of place, time, fortune, do cohere and jump
255   That I am Viola: which to confirm,
I'll bring you to a captain in this town,
Where lie my maiden weeds; by whose gentle help
I was preserved to serve this noble count.
All the occurrence of my fortune since
260   Hath been between this lady and this lord.

SEBASTIAN: [To Olivia] So comes it, lady, you have been mistook:
But nature to her bias drew in that.
You would have been contracted to a maid;

VIOLA: *I am from Messaline. Sebastian was my father, and I had a brother named Sebastian, too. He drowned wearing clothes like yours. If ghosts can take on bodies and clothes, you have come to frighten us.*

SEBASTIAN: *I am a spirit, indeed, but of the physical world I was born into. If you were a woman, since everything else indicates you are my sister, I would cry on your cheek and say, "Welcome, welcome, welcome, drowned Viola!"*

VIOLA: *My father had a mole on his forehead.*

SEBASTIAN: *So did mine.*

VIOLA: *He died the day of Viola's thirteenth birthday.*

SEBASTIAN: *Oh, that memory is clear in my mind! He did die on my sister's thirteenth birthday.*

VIOLA: *If nothing prevents us from being happy, other than my masculine clothing, do not hug me until every detail of place, time, and fate falls together to prove that I am Viola. I can confirm this by bringing you to a captain in this town, who has my woman's clothing. Through his kind help, I was saved and brought to serve this noble count. My life since then has been dedicated to this lady and this lord.*

SEBASTIAN: *[To Olivia.] This is how you have been mistaken, lady, but nature has turned it in your favor. You would have been married to a*

Nor are you therein, by my life, deceived,
265   You are betroth'd both to a maid and man.

DUKE ORSINO: Be not amazed; right noble is his blood.
If this be so, as yet the glass seems true,
I shall have share in this most happy wreck.
[To Viola] Boy, thou hast said to me a thousand times
270   Thou never shouldst love woman like to me.

VIOLA: And all those sayings will I overswear;
And those swearings keep as true in soul
As doth that orbed continent the fire
That severs day from night.

275 DUKE ORSINO: Give me thy hand;
And let me see thee in thy woman's weeds.

VIOLA: The captain that did bring me first on shore
Hath my maid's garments: he upon some action
Is now in durance, at Malvolio's suit,
280   A gentleman, and follower of my lady's.

OLIVIA: He shall enlarge him: fetch Malvolio hither:
And yet, alas, now I remember me,
They say, poor gentleman, he's much distract.

[Re-enter Clown with a letter, and Fabian]
A most extracting frenzy of mine own
285   From my remembrance clearly banish'd his.
How does he, sirrah?

CLOWN: Truly, madam, he holds Belzebub at the staves's end as
well as a man in his case may do: has here writ a letter to
you; I should have given't you to-day morning, but as a
290   madman's epistles are no gospels, so it skills not much when
they are delivered.

OLIVIA: Open 't, and read it.

woman; therefore, by my life, you are not deceived. Now you are married to both a virgin and a man.

DUKE: Do not be dismayed. He is of noble blood. If this is true, as it seems to be, I will take part in this happy disaster. [To Viola.] Boy, you have said to me a thousand times that you would never love a woman as much as you love me.

VIOLA: I would swear to it again for each time I said it. In addition, I would honor all those oaths as faithfully as the sun rises and sets each day.

DUKE: Give me your hand, and let me see you in your woman's clothes.

VIOLA: The captain who first brought me to shore has my clothes. He is imprisoned over some suit that Malvolio, a gentleman and my lady's servant, began.

OLIVIA: He will release him. Bring Malvolio here. Oh, but now I remember, they say he has gone mad, the poor gentleman.

[Re-enter Feste, a Clown with a letter, and Fabian.] I completely forgot about this because of my own distracting agitation. How is he, sir?

CLOWN: Truly, madam, he is fighting off Satan as well as a man in his situation can. He has written a letter to you. I should have given it to you this morning, but, since a madman's letters are not gospels, it does not really matter when they are delivered.

OLIVIA: Open it, and read it.

CLOWN: Look then to be well edified when the fool delivers the madman. *[Reads]* 'By the Lord, madam,'—

295 OLIVIA: How now! art thou mad?

CLOWN: No, madam, I do but read madness: an your ladyship will have it as it ought to be, you must allow Vox.

OLIVIA: Prithee, read i' thy right wits.

CLOWN: So I do, madonna; but to read his right wits is to
300   read thus: therefore perpend, my princess, and give ear.

OLIVIA: Read it you, sirrah.   *[To Fabian]*

FABIAN: *[Reads]* 'By the Lord, madam, you wrong me, and the world shall know it: though you have put me into darkness and given your drunken cousin rule over me, yet have I the benefit of my
305   senses as well as your ladyship. I have your own letter that induced me to the semblance I put on; with the which I doubt not but to do myself much right, or you much shame. Think of me as you please. I leave my duty a little unthought of and speak out of my injury.
              THE MADLY-USED MALVOLIO.

310 OLIVIA: Did he write this?

CLOWN: Ay, madam.

DUKE ORSINO: This savours not much of distraction.

OLIVIA: See him deliver'd, Fabian; bring him hither.
                            [Exit Fabian]
    My lord so please you, these things further thought on,
315   To think me as well a sister as a wife,
    One day shall crown the alliance on't, so please you,
    Here at my house and at my proper cost.

CLOWN: *Expect to be very much enlightened when I read what the madman has written.* [Reads.] *By the Lord, madam—*

OLIVIA: *What! Are you mad?*

CLOWN: *No, madam, I am only reading the madness. If you want to hear it, as it should be read, you must allow me to use my voice.*

OLIVIA: *I beg you, read it like a normal person.*

CLOWN: *I am, my lady. However, to read his right mind is to read it like this. Therefore, think carefully, my princess, and listen.*

OLIVIA: [To Fabian.] *You read it, fellow.*

FABIAN: [Reads.] *By the lord, madam, you are doing me wrong, and the world will know it. Although you have put me into darkness and let your drunken cousin rule over me, I am still as sane as you are. I have your own letter that urged me to act the way I did, which will show that I am in the right and put you to shame. Think of me how you want. I am being rude, but I speak out of the injustice that has been done to me.*
                    THE MADLY-USED MALVOLIO

OLIVIA: *Did he write this?*

CLOWN: *Yes, madam.*

DUKE: *This does not seem like madness.*

OLIVIA: *Let him out, Fabian. Bring him here.*   [Exit Fabian.]
    My lord, if it is pleasing to you, once you think these things through, I hope you will accept me as a sister-in-law instead of a wife. If you accept, we will marry on one day, here at my house, and I will pay for it.

DUKE ORSINO: Madam, I am most apt to embrace your offer.
    [To Viola] Your master quits you; and for your service done
320   him,
    So much against the mettle of your sex,
    So far beneath your soft and tender breeding,
    And since you call'd me master for so long,
    Here is my hand: you shall from this time be
325   Your master's mistress.

OLIVIA: A sister! you are she.

[Re-enter Fabian, with Malvolio]

DUKE ORSINO: Is this the madman?

OLIVIA: Ay, my lord, this same.
    How now, Malvolio!

330 MALVOLIO: Madam, you have done me wrong,
    Notorious wrong.

OLIVIA: Have I, Malvolio? no.

MALVOLIO: Lady, you have. Pray you, peruse that letter.
    You must not now deny it is your hand:
335   Write from it, if you can, in hand or phrase;
    Or say 'tis not your seal, nor your invention:
    You can say none of this: well, grant it then
    And tell me, in the modesty of honour,
    Why you have given me such clear lights of favour,
340   Bade me come smiling and cross-garter'd to you,
    To put on yellow stockings and to frown
    Upon Sir Toby and the lighter people;
    And, acting this in an obedient hope,
    Why have you suffer'd me to be imprison'd,
345   Kept in a dark house, visited by the priest,
    And made the most notorious geck and gull
    That e'er invention play'd on? tell me why.

DUKE: *Madam, I am pleased to accept your offer.* [To Viola.] *Your master lets you go. For the service you have done him, so unwomanly and beneath your noble upbringing, and since you have called me master for so long, here is my hand. You will from now on be your master's mistress.*

OLIVIA: *A sister! You are one.*

[Re-enter Fabian with Malvolio.]

DUKE: *Is this the madman?*

OLIVIA: *Yes, my lord, the same one. How are you, Malvolio!*

MALVOLIO: *Madam, you have done me wrong, notorious wrong.*

OLIVIA: *Have I, Malvolio? No.*

MALVOLIO: *Lady, you have. Please, look over this letter. You cannot deny now that it is in your handwriting. Write differently from it, if you can, in handwriting or style. Or, say it does not have your seal, the one you created. You cannot say any of this. Well, confirm it then, and tell me, truthfully, why you have given me hints that you cared for me. You asked me to come smiling and cross-gartered to you, and to put on yellow stockings and look down on Sir Toby and lesser people. Tell me why, when I did this hopefully and obediently, you let me be imprisoned, kept in a dark room, visited by the priest, and made the most notorious idiot and simpleton that ever was tricked? Tell me why.*

OLIVIA: Alas, Malvolio, this is not my writing,
Though, I confess, much like the character
350　But out of question 'tis Maria's hand.
And now I do bethink me, it was she
First told me thou wast mad; then camest in smiling,
And in such forms which here were presupposed
Upon thee in the letter. Prithee, be content:
355　This practise hath most shrewdly pass'd upon thee;
But when we know the grounds and authors of it,
Thou shalt be both the plaintiff and the judge
Of thine own cause.

FABIAN: Good madam, hear me speak,
360　And let no quarrel nor no brawl to come
Taint the condition of this present hour,
Which I have wonder'd at. In hope it shall not,
Most freely I confess, myself and Toby
Set this device against Malvolio here,
365　Upon some stubborn and uncourteous parts
We had conceived against him: Maria writ
The letter at Sir Toby's great importance;
In recompense whereof he hath married her.
How with a sportful malice it was follow'd,
370　May rather pluck on laughter than revenge;
If that the injuries be justly weigh'd
That have on both sides pass'd.

OLIVIA: Alas, poor fool, how have they baffled thee!

CLOWN: Why, 'some are born great, some achieve greatness, and
375　some have greatness thrown upon them.' I was one, sir, in
this interlude; one Sir Topas, sir; but that's all one. 'By the
Lord, fool, I am not mad.' But do you remember? 'Madam,
why laugh you at such a barren rascal? an you smile not, he's
gagged:' and thus the whirligig of time brings in his revenges.

380　MALVOLIO: I'll be revenged on the whole pack of you. *[Exit]*

OLIVIA: *Oh, Malvolio, this is not my handwriting. Although I admit it is very similar, it is definitely Maria's handwriting. Now that I think about it, she first told me that you were mad. Then you came in smiling, dressed, and behaving in the way the letter told you to. Please, be certain, this joke has been played upon you very skillfully, but when we know who thought it up and executed it, you will be both the plaintiff and the judge of your own case.*

FABIAN: *Good madam, listen to me, and do not let arguing or future fight ruin the joy of this present time, by which I have been amazed. I hope it will not. I very openly confess that Toby and I have played this trick upon Malvolio, because we were offended by his rude and condescending attitude. Maria wrote the letter because Sir Toby insisted on it, and, in return for her help, he has married her. Describing how the trick was executed with playful cruelty would probably cause more laughter than want for revenge, especially if the complaints from both sides are fairly compared.*

OLIVIA: *Oh, you poor fool, how they have ridiculed you!*

CLOWN: *Why, "some are born great, some achieve greatness, and some have greatness thrown upon them." I participated in this trick. I was Sir Topas, sir, but that is all the same. "By the Lord, fool, I am not mad." But do you remember? "Madam, why do you laugh at such a stupid rascal? Unless you laugh and urge him on, he falls silent." In this way, the spinning top of time brings revenge.*

MALVOLIO: *I will take revenge upon the whole group of you.* [He exits.]

OLIVIA: He hath been most notoriously abused.

DUKE ORSINO: Pursue him and entreat him to a peace:
He hath not told us of the captain yet:
When that is known and golden time convents,
385   A solemn combination shall be made
Of our dear souls. Meantime, sweet sister,
We will not part from hence. Cesario, come;
For so you shall be, while you are a man;
But when in other habits you are seen,
390   Orsino's mistress and his fancy's queen.

[Exeunt all, except Clown]

CLOWN: *[Sings]*
        When that I was and a little tiny boy,
          With hey, ho, the wind and the rain,
        A foolish thing was but a toy,
395   For the rain it raineth every day.

        But when I came to man's estate,
          With hey, ho, & c.
        'Gainst knaves and thieves men shut their gate,
          For the rain, & c.

400   But when I came, alas! to wive,
          With hey, ho, & c.
        By swaggering could I never thrive,
          For the rain, & c.

        But when I came unto my beds,
405   With hey, ho, & c.
        With toss-pots still had drunken heads,
          For the rain, & c.

        A great while ago the world begun,
          With hey, ho, & c.
410   But that's all one, our play is done,
          And we'll strive to please you every day.

[Exit]

OLIVIA: *He has been most shamefully mistreated.*

DUKE: *Follow him, and make peace with him. He has not told us about the captain yet. When that is confirmed, and the golden time arrives, a solemn alliance will be made between our dear souls. In the meantime, sweet sister, we will not leave here. Cesario, come here, because that is what I will call you while you are still dressed like a man. However, when I see you in other clothes, you will be my wife and the queen of my love.*

[Everyone exits, except Feste, a Clown.]

CLOWN: [Sings]

When that I was and a little tiny boy,
    With hey, ho, the wind and the rain,
A foolish thing was but a toy,
    For the rain it raineth every day.

But when I came to man's estate,
    With hey, ho, the wind and the rain,
'Gainst knaves and thieves men shut their gate,
    For the rain it raineth every day.

But when I came, alas! to wive,
    With hey, ho, the wind and the rain,
By swaggering could I never thrive,
    For the rain it raineth every day.

But when I came unto my beds,
    With hey, ho, the wind and the rain,
With toss-pots still had drunken heads,
    For the rain it raineth everyday.

A great while ago the world begun,
    With hey, ho, the wind and the rain,
But that's all one, our play is done,
    And we'll strive to please you every day.

[He exits.]

STUDY GUIDE

Act I, Scene 1

How would you describe the Duke based on his behavior in this scene? Use specific examples to support your description.

Act I, Scene 2

What plan, involving the Captain, does Viola devise? What reasons do you think she has for coming up with such a plan?

Act I, Scene 3

What is your first impression of Sir Andrew and Sir Toby? Why is Sir Andrew spending time in Sir Toby's company?

Act I, Scene 4

Why does the Duke think Viola/Cesario will do a good job bringing his message of love to Olivia? What secret reason does Viola have for not wanting to flatter Olivia on behalf of the Duke?

Act I, Scene 5

There are many times throughout the play when Viola/ Cesario hints that she is in disguise to Olivia. Find one in this scene, and explain its meaning.

Act II, Scene 1

How has Antonio helped Sebastian? How does he again take a risk by following Sebastian?

Act II, Scene 2

Why has Olivia sent Malvolio after Cesario? Describe the complicated love triangle that now exists.

Act II, Scene 3

What is the substance of the disagreement between Sir Toby and Malvolio? Explain both of their perspectives.

Act II, Scene 4

Define dramatic irony. Explain the dramatic irony that occurs in this scene between the Duke and Viola.

Act II, Scene 5

Explain the trick Maria, Sir Toby, and the others play on Malvolio. How does Malvolio react to it?

Act III, Scene I

What is the primary purpose of this scene?

Act III, Scene 2

Why is Sir Andrew threatening to leave Illyria? How does Sir Toby suggest that Andrew remedy the situation?

Act III, Scene 3

Why do Sebastian and Antonio go separate ways?

Act III, Scene 4

How does Sir Toby deceive both Sir Andrew and Viola? What happens when Antonio encounters Viola?

Act IV, Scene 1

What drives Sebastian to say, "Are all the people mad?" (IV, i)How does Olivia intervene?

Act IV, Scene 2

How do Maria and Sir Toby further torment Malvolio during this scene? Do you think Malvolio deserves this treatment, or has it gone too far? Explain why you think so.

Act IV, Scene 3

How does Sebastian explain his encounter with Olivia? What do they plan to do?

Act V, Scene I

The play resolves with three marriages or plans for marriages. Who gets married, and which characters are left out of the happy ending?